The No-Nonsense, Real-Life Guide to Estate Planning In Canada

Lynne Butler, BA LLB TEP

Copyright © 2016 by Lynne Butler

All rights reserved. This book or any portion thereof may not be reproduced or used in any manner whatsoever without the express written permission of the publisher except for the use of brief quotations in a book review or scholarly journal.

First printing: 2016

estatelawcanada@gmail.com

TABLE OF CONTENTS

Introduction	1
Chapter 1: Taking Stock – Your Family	7
A. Your current spouse – married vs common law	8
B. Dependent relief	13
C. Your former spouse	15
D. Minor children	16
E. Disabled children	17
F. Adopted children	20
G. Step children	21
H. Estranged children	23
I. Other dependents	25
Chapter 2: Taking Stock - Assets and liabilities	27
A. Real estate	28
B. Digital assets	29
C. Bank accounts and investments	32
D. Pensions	35
E. Liabilities	36
Chapter 3: Defining Your Goals	39
A. Look after spouse	40
B. Equally among children	40
C. Equal vs fair	43
D. Advances to your children	45
E. Balance a blended family	47
F. Leave a legacy	49
G. Keep land in the family	52
H. Hand down the family business	57
I. Intestacy	59

Chapter 4: Estate Documents — 77
- A. Will — 78
- B. Handwritten will — 84
- C. Codicil — 87
- D. Enduring Power of Attorney — 88
- E. Healthcare Directive — 99
- F. Memorandum to executor — 101
- G. Memorandum of Personal Effects — 102
- H. Shareholders' agreement — 106

Chapter 5: Understanding Your Personal Estate Plan Puzzle — 109
- A. Designated beneficiaries — 111
- B. Registered Education Savings Plan (RESP) — 113
- C. Life insurance — 114
- D. Joint property — 116
- E. Intergenerational joint property — 119
- F. Divorce or separation — 124
- G. Prenuptial agreement — 126
- H. Matrimonial home — 128

Chapter 6: Trusts — 137
- A. Minor children — 138
- B. Disabled child — 147
- C. Spendthrift — 150
- D. Creditor protection — 151
- E. Blended families — 152
- F. Income splitting — 155
- G. Keeping the inheritance away from the in-laws — 156

Chapter 7: Taxation	159
A. Capital gains tax	161
B. Principal residence exemption	163
C. Farm rollover	164
D. Personal lifetime exemption	165
E. Income tax	166
F. Probate fee/tax	168
Chapter 8: Tips for a Better Will	171
A. Executor compensation	171
B. Public policy restrictions	175
C. Contemplation of marriage	178
D. Instructions for your remains	182
E. Asking the impossible	184
F. Where do you leave your estate if you have no children?	186
Chapter 9: Getting Advice	193
A. Lawyer	194
B. Accountant	201
C. Financial advisor	204
Chapter 10: Probate	207
A. Facts about probate	207
B. Cost of probate	211
C. Avoiding probate	215
D. Why avoid probate?	216
E. Weighing the risks against the benefits	217
F. Survivorship presumptions	221
Conclusion	227
Estate Planning Worksheet	229
More Books by Lynne Butler	243

LIST OF TABLES:

Table 1:	Common law right of inheritance in all provinces and territories in Canada	11
Table 2:	Distribution on intestacy in all provinces and territories in Canada	61
Table 3:	Jurisdictions across Canada that allow holographic wills	86
Table 4:	Treatment of matrimonial home on the death of one spouse in all provinces and territories in Canada	129
Table 5:	Revocation of wills upon marriage and divorce in all provinces and territories in Canada	179
Table 6:	Cost of probate across Canada	211
Table 7:	Survivorship presumptions in all provinces and territories in Canada	223

INTRODUCTION

From time to time, people tell me that they find the phrase "estate planning" to be a bit lofty for them and that it doesn't really apply to them. They believe that because their assets are modest, they aren't really planning an estate but are simply getting a will made. To me, that's just a matter of semantics. Having a will is the result of your planning – or lack of it - whether or not you think of it that way. If your planning is haphazard or incomplete, your will is going to reflect that.

Planning an estate for an ordinary Canadian whose assets amount to a few thousand dollars is just as important as planning one for a multi-millionaire celebrity. Estate planning is not just about passing on huge mansions or massive trust funds; it's about making the most of what you have worked hard to gain, and ensuring that it passes to your family without fights, delays, or extra costs. Everyone who wants to ensure a smooth estate and to preserve family harmony should plan ahead.

The purpose of this book is to provide you with information that will help you make solid decisions. It will guide you through topics that are relevant to everyone who is thinking about having a will made or about updating a current will. This book is not just about wills, though. It will also cover planning for the possible onset of mental incapacity due to age, illness, or injury. It will also encourage you to think about your estate plan as a group of items that includes your will as well as other financial and legal arrangements such as life insurance, RRSPs, and divorce settlements. Everything needs to work together to avoid nasty surprises.

In addition, this book will talk about topics that affect your planning that you may not have thought about, such as taxation, gifts of money to your adult kids, and blended families.

Throughout the book, I have drawn on my thirty years as a wills lawyer and former estates paralegal to point out and describe mistakes that people frequently make, to the detriment of those left behind. It's very easy to make serious errors simply because information found in magazines and particularly online is often reduced to a list of brief tips, incorrect, out of date, or intended for an audience in another province or country. I hope to alert you to those potential mistakes and to give you some ideas about better ways to attain your estate-planning goals.

Many readers will see within the pages of this book some steps they have seen discussed in magazines, newspapers, books, and webpages. My advice on any given topic may or may not be the same as the advice you have seen before, but my explanations and examples should be extensive enough to see why I have given the advice I have. Some of you will realize that you've already made some of the errors that are covered here. Hopefully you'll get new ideas about how to achieve the goals you want to meet, and some insight as to the dangers of steps you may already have taken.

This guide is called "no-nonsense" and "real-life" for one very good reason. It's based on years of practical experience with solving real problems for real people, and not on academic theory. It doesn't seek to dazzle you with complicated legal terms or to bore you with the history of how things ended up the way they are. This book is about getting things done properly and sensibly, and making informed choices.

This book is for people who want information they can read without needing a legal dictionary at their side, and who also want the most up-to-date and accurate information available.

All of Canada's laws dealing with wills, estates, probate, and related matters are made by the provinces and not by the federal government. This means that the law varies quite a bit from one province to the next. The differences between provinces can be surprisingly large, particularly with respect to far-reaching matters such as common law rights. In this book I have made every effort to be clear that while the legal concepts apply to all of us in all parts of the country, the mechanics of the law (such as forms, procedures, costs, processes, and rules) are different in each province and territory.

Where information varies from province to province, such as the cost of applying to the court for probate, I have included a reference table that summarizes the law in each province and territory. There are several such tables provided in this book. This should be useful to readers who can check to find out immediately what applies to them, rather than reading general statements about what "most places" do in that situation. Be sure to refer to these tables as you go through the chapters so that you know for sure how the law is going to impact you and your family.

The law of wills and estates is always in transition as governments pass new statutes to reflect changing public standards and ideas. The core foundation of wills law stays the same, while the ways and means of carrying out the wishes of an individual change. In this book, I have ensured that all legislative updates in all provinces have been included so that this book contains the very latest and most accurate information available.

My goal in preparing this guide is to give information that people can understand and put to use in their own planning. My clients, as well as those who attend my seminars and the millions of people who have read my blog know that I take a practical approach. I keep the realities of people's lives – both their strengths and their failings – in mind as I address their questions and help them find answers. I want to help make readers into better prepared and more informed consumers of legal services.

At the end of this book, you will find an Estate Planning Worksheet. When you're ready to begin your estate planning, you may use the Worksheet as your first step. Use it to gather your thoughts and collect relevant data. You'll save a lot of time at the lawyer's office if you go in with your material organized and ready. You'll also feel more prepared and focused.

Following the Estate Planning Worksheet, you will see other books I have written and kits I have prepared to assist individuals with their planning, as well as their estate administration. Feel free to browse through the selection, and to call my office if you need some guidance as to which books would assist you.

Finally, please drop by my blog at www.estatelawcanada.blogspot.ca to find out more about many of the topics discussed in this book. You can leave comments, ask questions, or give feedback on any estate-related matter that interests you.

CHAPTER 1: TAKING STOCK – YOUR FAMILY

The first step toward putting together an estate plan, whether simple or complex, is to take stock of your situation. Where do things stand financially and personally? What are the specific facts of your life that need to be taken into consideration? Who do you want to look after, and who will have a possible claim against your estate? Take the time to think about who and what is involved in your unique life.

Your family is the starting point for all estate planning, no matter how large, small, complex, or simple your family may be. Your family situation shapes your goals and raises issues for you to overcome. As you read through this chapter, consider your own family and how its unique formation fits together with your goals. No doubt you will be taken by surprise by a few of the points made, as most people don't really think of their own situations as being complicated.

These days, families come in all shapes and sizes. Even if your family is a tangle of marriages, step-children, and inter-generational households, it can all be addressed by a good, solid estate plan as long as you take the time to form realistic goals and take sensible steps to achieve them.

There are things about your family – about everyone's families – that are important in the context of estate planning. In your case, there could be a step-child, an aging parent, or someone with a disability that you want to look after. There could be an estranged sibling, a family business, or a cottage that everyone in the family uses.

These are the things you may not think to mention to an estate planner or lawyer but will affect your estate in the end. As you go through this book and the chapters and concepts become more complex, you'll see why these issues are important.

A. Your current spouse – married vs. common law

Because your spouse is your next of kin, let's start the review of your family there. The first question to answer about your spouse is whether you are legally married or living in a common law relationship. While many people believe that common law spouses have the same rights as married spouses, this is not necessarily the case. In fact, in some provinces, common law spouses have zero right to inherit anything in the absence of a will. The law varies widely between the provinces, and Table 1 below summarizes the position of common law spouses across Canada.

It is a serious mistake to assume that a common law spouse has inheritance rights, even if that same person is treated as a spouse for other purposes such as child maintenance, taxes, or pension. If you are in a common law relationship, make sure you check the table to see whether your relationship gives you inheritance rights in your province.

If you live in a jurisdiction which does not recognize common law marriages in terms of inheritance, you must ensure that you and your spouse plan ahead to protect each other. Remember that when the law says there are no inheritance rights, it means *in the absence of a will*, you do not have any claim against the estate. You can still inherit what your spouse leaves you in his or her will. It's essential that common law couples make wills to protect each other and their children.

In addition, common law couples should take special care with the title to their home. If they hold the home as joint owners, this means that when one of them passes away, the other one will own the home by right of survivorship. While this is how most couples, married or otherwise, set up their titles, it is even more important for common law couples. In some provinces, spouses get special rights to the matrimonial home on the death of their partner, and in others they don't. It's best to plan ahead so that neither of you is at risk of losing the home to other beneficiaries if your spouse passes away. The last thing you'd need immediately after the death of your spouse is a notice saying that you must immediately vacate your home.

Common law couples can also protect each other and their estates by using beneficiary designations that keep assets outside of their estates. For example, a man in a common law relationship could buy an insurance policy and name his common law wife as the beneficiary. She could open an RRSP and name her common law husband as her beneficiary. Those assets will pass to the named beneficiary (assuming he or she is still alive) regardless of whether they are legally married or living common law.

Another area in which unmarried couples can run into problems is that of incapacity. When an individual begins to suffer mental incapacity due to age, illness, injury, or medication, the next of kin is usually called upon to handle both medical and financial matters. In a legal marriage, the common law spouse is the next of kin. If you live in a jurisdiction where common law marriage is not recognized, there could be a problem. You might be forced to stand by silently while your partner's parents or siblings call the shots about your partner's medical treatment. If your relationship with the family is particularly amiable, you might not end up in this situation, but it's not unheard of for a family to dislike either an opposite-sex or same-sex common law partner. It is foolish to rely on the goodwill of others when you can ensure your position by putting the right documents in place.

To avoid this unpleasant scenario, individuals in common law relationships need to plan ahead for incapacity. They need to think about who they would want to put in charge if they could no longer make their own decisions. They may wish to name each other as the person who would instruct a doctor about end of life matters, or who would handle the finances and property. This involves preparing an Enduring Power of Attorney and a healthcare directive. In chapter 4 of this book you will find more details about these documents.

In summary, common law couples should:
- Make wills that leave assets to each other, and possibly to their children;
- Consider using joint title to their home;
- Consider using beneficiary designations to leave assets directly to each other;
- Plan for incapacity by preparing Enduring Powers of attorney and healthcare directives that name each other.

Table 1: *Common law right of inheritance across Canada in the absence of a will*

Province or territory	Inheritance rights held by common law spouse where his or her deceased spouse did not leave a will. **Note that this table only discusses common law in the context of _inheritance_ and NOT in the context of other matters such as child support or taxes.**
Alberta	Same as married spouse if you have lived together for at least 3 years. May displace married spouse under certain circumstances. After 3 years, you have the same right as married spouses for dependents' relief.
British Columbia	You are considered common law partners for the purpose of inheritance if you have lived in a marriage-like relationship for 2 years. After 2 years, you would have the right to request dependents' relief.
Manitoba	You are considered common law partners if you have lived in a conjugal relationship for 3 years, or for 1 year if you have a child together. After the appropriate amount of time, you have the right to request dependents' relief.

New Brunswick	None on inheritance. You may request dependents' relief.
Newfoundland & Labrador	None on inheritance. No right to request dependents' relief.
Northwest Territories	Same as a married spouse if you have lived together for at least 2 years in a relationship of some permanence, or a shorter time if you are the natural or adoptive parents of a child together.
Nova Scotia	No right on inheritance unless you have signed a domestic partnership agreement. If the agreement is signed, your rights are the same as a married spouse. Without the agreement, as a common law spouse you have no right to inherit. No right to request dependents' relief unless the agreement is signed.
Nunavut	Same as a married spouse if you have lived together for at least 2 years in a relationship of some permanence, or a shorter time if you are the natural or adoptive parents of a child together.
Ontario	None on inheritance. You may request dependents' relief.
Prince Edward Island	None on inheritance. No right to claim dependents' relief.
Quebec	None on inheritance. No right to claim dependent's relief.

Saskatchewan	Same as a married spouse if you have lived together for at least 2 years.
Yukon	Same as married spouse.

B. Dependents' relief

Every province and territory in Canada has a law that confirms that your spouse is your dependent. Because the spouse is a dependent, if you pass away, you do not have the option to leave your spouse out of your will. This doesn't mean that the will document could not be made, only that it is almost guaranteed to be contested unless you and your spouse have agreed that your spouse is not going to receive anything under your will. You could make a valid will without including your spouse, but you should be aware that the law frowns on this and it is pretty easy for a spouse to contest your will and be awarded a share of (or all of) your estate. You are legally required to address your dependents' needs. These laws are generally referred to as "dependent relief" or "family relief" laws because they are aimed at ensuring that on the death of an individual, his or her spouse and children are not left destitute while somebody else receives the estate.

Dependent relief law gives a spouse the right to contest a will where he or she is not given enough of the estate, or where there was no will and the spouse did not get the whole estate. The right arises automatically because of the legal contract of marriage. Again, this can be a major difference between a legal marriage and a common law relationship. These rules don't always apply to common law spouses. Check the table above to find out where a common law spouse stands in your province.

Summary:
The people in your life who have an automatic right to support under your will under dependents' relief law in all parts of Canada are:
- Your spouse
- Your minor children
- Your disabled children, regardless of age

In Alberta, there are two additional groups of people who also have the same right to dependents' relief as against your estate. One group would include your adult children who are under the age of 22 years and who are in school full time. The other group would include your minor grandchildren or great grandchildren if you were raising them in place of their parent.

Individuals who are married usually do leave their estates to each other, but not always. Sometimes people wish to leave money or other property directly to their children or to charitable organizations, or to other individuals, with only a portion of the estate going to their spouse. This is particularly true of blended families. There is more information about blended families in chapter 3.

Whenever a married person (and in some cases a person in a common law relationship) makes a will in which his or her spouse is going to receive less than the full estate, that person needs to realize that the spouse can claim against the estate to get the whole thing, even when this means the children won't receive anything at the time. This is because in most places, the dependent relief law allows the spouse to claim for as much of the estate as he or she thinks is needed to support him or her.

Many individuals don't find that the existence of the dependent relief law with respect to their spouse changes their plans in any way. They have discussed their plans with their spouses and both parties are agreed that some portion of the estate may be left elsewhere without the danger of it being contested. It's a leap of faith in which the spouses promise not to contest each other's estates, without actually imposing a legal obligation on each other.

C. Your former spouse

Generally speaking, former spouses themselves don't have a huge impact on estates, as long as in the case of divorce, the matrimonial property has been divided between the parties and is all settled. If you should pass away before this division has been completed, your former spouse may have a claim against your estate for the value of any matrimonial property that has not yet been divided. A claim like that would have priority over anything you leave to individuals in your will. This is a good reason not to let divorce issues linger on for any longer than necessary.

If you have been widowed, check your paperwork to see whether you have removed your spouse's name from the title to your assets, particularly of your home. If you have not done so and you pass away while the title still shows that you both own the property, your executor may have to probate your will and then go back and probate your former spouse's will as well. This can cause delays and extra costs, particularly if many years have passed and your spouse's will is no longer available. You can avoid this problem simply by taking care of the update of the title yourself while you are alive.

D. Minor children

Minor children are the focus of a lot of attention during the estate planning process because they are dependents, and because they cannot inherit until they reach adulthood. In addition to trying to protect funds that are left for minor children, parents also have to try to name someone they trust to actually raise their children as well. It's a very tough decision for many parents. All of this means that there is usually a great deal of planning on the part of parents to get the care and support of minor children just right.

Because minor children are dependents, they automatically have the right to be supported by their parents' estates. This means that if parents don't make proper arrangements for their minor children, those children (through a trustee or advocate) may sue the estate for better support. This is part of the dependent's relief legislation that was discussed above. If there is nobody else to represent a minor child, the provincial Office of the Public Trustee will usually step in to oversee the child's interest in the estate.

If you are paying child support according to a separation agreement, maintenance agreement, or divorce decree, the responsibility for that support will continue on even after you pass away. In other words, if you pass away while a minor child who is dependent on you is only, say, eight years old, your estate will be responsible for paying the support that you would have paid until the child attains the age of majority.

Realistically, it's impractical for an estate to stay open for that many years to satisfy the child support requirements. Instead, your executor should calculate the amount of support remaining on your agreement or order and set that aside. Whoever is representing the minor child will work with the executor to reach an agreement on what the amount should be. There is generally some negotiating because not all child support benefits are fully defined. For example, there is usually an agreement for the parents to split "extra" costs in addition to the regular monthly payments. Once the amount has been agreed upon, your executor will pay that amount to the child's representative in exchange for a full release of that obligation. Then the executor can get on with the rest of the estate.

The share of your estate that goes to a minor child must be held in trust until that child reaches the age of majority. You have the choice to pick a later age than the age of majority if you want to. In fact, when you make a will, you have many ways of controlling or directing the share of a minor child so that the share is protected and used in the way you think best for the child. See chapter 6 about trusts to get further ideas about how you can deal with the share of a minor.

E. Disabled children

A disabled child is in a similar position to a minor child in that he or she is a legal dependent of his or her parent. The major difference is that a minor child will eventually become an adult and cease to be a dependent whereas a disabled child is usually considered to be a dependent for his or her entire lifetime.

Therefore, a parent must make special arrangements for the care of a disabled child that he or she would likely not make for his or her other children.

Because a disabled child is a dependent, he or she has the same automatic right to dependent relief from an estate that has been mentioned above for spouses and minor children. A parent who does not adequately provide for a disabled child should expect the estate to be challenged by the dependent child's trustee or advocate.

Most parents want to treat their children equally in their wills if they can, but they realize that when a disabled child is involved, that may not be possible. If the parent's estate is large enough so that a disabled child who receives an equal share is well looked after, there is no reason for the disabled child to receive more than his or her siblings. On the other hand, if the estate is more modest, it might be necessary for the parent to leave more of the estate to the disabled child and less to the other children.

The share of a physically disabled child does not necessarily have to be held in trust. If the disability is purely physical and does not impair the child's ability to deal with finances, his or her share may be paid to him or her upon reaching adulthood just as it would with any other child. On the other hand, when a disability – either a mental disability or a severe physical disability - does impair the child's ability to deal with finances, his or her share will be held in trust, usually for the child's entire lifetime.

Most parents choose to create a trust that looks after their disabled child for his or her entire life, and to specify who is to look after the money. A trust like this would deal with any money that is left over at the end of the disabled child's life. It can go anywhere that the parents wish, as the trust for the child is completely governed by the parents' wills. A popular idea is to divide any unused funds among the siblings of the disabled child.

Many disabled individuals, upon reaching adulthood, will qualify for provincial government disability benefits that replace or supplement income and provide financial assistance. The plans also include free medical, dental, and optical care. To most individuals who receive these benefits, they are extremely valuable and very much needed. This fact creates the need for careful planning for the simple reason that the provincial plans administer both a means test and an assets test to the recipients of the benefits. If the recipient has more money than the maximum amount allowed (and in some provinces it is extremely low) then the recipient is cut off from the benefits.

The idea behind leaving funds to a disabled person in a will is to make their lives easier, not harder, so it is important to figure out how to leave an inheritance without disturbing the provincial benefits.

To avoid forcing disabled individuals off the provincial benefits, estate planning lawyers will help the parents of the disabled individual by creating a trust in their wills that will hold the inheritance in such a way that it does not affect the benefits program. In Canada this type of trust is called a Henson Trust. See chapter 6 about trusts to learn more about Henson Trusts and how they are used to support disabled beneficiaries.

F. Adopted children

A child who has been adopted is the legal child of his or her adoptive parents for all legal purposes, including inheritance. An adopted child has exactly the same rights as the biological child of the adoptive parents. When a person makes a will that says to share the estate among "my children" this means all of the biological and adopted children.

Adoptive situations can sometimes give rise to questions, particularly where a child who was given up for adoption later finds his or her biological parents and they develop a strong relationship. In many cases, when the biological parent passes away, the child believes that he or she should be part of the family that shares the deceased's estate because he or she has been reunited with the biological parent.

However, if the parent who gave up the child for adoption does not leave a will, or leaves a will that simply refers to "my children", that does not include the child that was given up for adoption. Even if the parent has since developed a wonderful, loving relationship with the child he or she gave up, the law does not change.

This doesn't mean that a biological parent who gave up a child cannot leave a gift to the child; it means that in the absence of a specific mention in a valid will, the child is simply not involved. In order for a biological parent to leave something to a child that he or she gave up for adoption, the parent must specifically name the child in his or her will and describe what is to be given to the child. Keep in mind that the adoption severed the legal relationship between the parent and the child. The parent can leave something to the child just as he or she could leave something to any other friend, but the child has no automatic right to anything.

This can be an emotionally difficult situation for a child who has reunited with his or her birth parents after being adopted by someone else. If the birth parent died without leaving a will, the estate could be given to nieces or nephews rather than to the birth child. It doesn't feel right to some people in that situation because the emotional bond is strong. However, the law is concerned only with legal bonds and not so much with emotional ties.

G. Step-children

The traditional, nuclear family is no longer the most common family structure. These days, families are blended in many different ways, and as a result, many hundreds of thousands of Canadians have step-children. Step-children do not have the same legal standing as biological or adopted children in terms of inheritance law, so special steps must be taken to deal with them.

The existence of step-children in the family of a person who has passed away can be an issue for his or her estate if the deceased did not leave a will, or was not clear enough or specific enough in his or her will about who was to be included.

When a person passes away without a will, the law of his or her province or territory determines who gets what from his or her estate. Step-children are not part of that. They do not have any right at all to inherit from a step-parent unless that step-parent has legally adopted them. This means a formal adoption through the courts; taking a child into your family and treating him or her as your own does not create the legal relationship that entitles the child to a share of your estate.

When a person passes away leaving a will that gives his or her estate to "my children" that does not include step-children unless the person had adopted the step-children. However, that may not be the understanding of the family members left behind, and the lack of certainty may lead to disputes about who is actually meant to be included. If a step-parent passes away after raising a child for many years, the child and the rest of the family may expect that the child will be treated as a true child of the deceased. This type of dispute is emotionally extremely difficult and often results in families being split permanently.

Keep in mind that in a case like this, an executor does not have the right to change a will to "do what is right" and include step-children (or anyone else). The executor must do what's set out in the will. If there is no will, the administrator appointed by the court has to follow the province's intestacy law and give the estate to those who are legally entitled to it. Families often accuse executors or administrators of being unfair or cold or cruel by excluding a step-child, but the reality is that if the step-child is not mentioned by name in a valid will, that's not the fault of the executor.
If you have step-children and you want them to receive

something from your estate, make sure you address them directly in your will. Similarly, if you want to exclude step-children (or, as is much more common, step-grandchildren), address that specifically in your will as well.

H. Estranged children

From time to time, families end up with some members not speaking to each other. When this goes on for some time, the relationship between the family members is eventually lost, and the parties are said to be estranged. Sometimes this ends up being a permanent situation. Whatever the reason for a particular estrangement, it creates a situation in which the parents of an estranged child are not sure what they should do about that child in their wills. Some want to include the estranged child and some don't, but what they all have in common is that they want to avoid a dispute or will challenge by the estranged child.

As a general rule, parents are not required by law to provide anything in their wills to adult children who are not financially dependent on them. This means that you can leave an estranged child out of your will if you wish to do so, just as you can leave out a child from whom you are not estranged. However, it's a good idea to clarify your reasons for doing so, rather than just omitting to mention the person.

Case law in Canada has recently looked at some situations in which adult children who were estranged from their parents were left out of the parents' wills, and brought lawsuit to try to get a share of the estate. The courts se to be saying that as long as there was a logical reason for the parent to disown the child, it can be done. For example, in some wills, a parent made a statement along the lines that he or she was leaving a child out of the will because they hadn't spoken in years and the child wouldn't respond to requests for reconciliation. That seemed to the courts to be good reason for a parent to disown a child and the wills were allowed to stand as they were. The courts were generally not willing to force parents to leave some part of the estate to someone with whom they do not have a good relationship.

On the other hand, the court does not always allow the parent to leave out a child, depending on the reason given for leaving out a child. If the reason is for something that is against public policy, the courts have often overturned the wills. For example, the court may overturn a will that leaves out a child for being homosexual or for marrying someone from a different race. Anyone who makes a will based on this kind of reasoning is taking a chance that the child who is being left out could be successful in challenging the will.

In British Columbia, the law is somewhat different than the law in other provinces, in that it allows a child who is left out of a will to contest the will based on *fairness*. Basically the child claims that it's unfair that he or she received less than his or her siblings from the estate. Sometimes they are successful in their lawsuits.

I. **Other dependents**

Though estate law defines certain parties as always being a dependent – those parties being a spouse, a minor child, and an adult child with a disability that prevents the child from earning a living – it's possible that you have other dependents in your life as well. Families are complex these days, and it is not at all unusual to find various combinations of relatives living in one household.

For example, you could have an aging parent living with you, or a brother with a disability, or a niece who is attending university. Whether or not those individuals would qualify as your dependents would depend on the specific circumstances of your financial arrangements. If you are the sole supplier of income for a person and they have no other means of earning an income, then you should seriously consider whether you should make provision for them in your will. Making arrangements for them in your will could prevent them from challenging your will if they are left out.

Keep in mind that the arrangements you make for those you choose to support, such as an aging parent, may be flexible. For example, instead of giving a gift of money outright, you could benefit that person by leaving a sum of money in trust. They could use as much of the money as they need. Any money that is left over would then go back to your estate and be divided among your children or whoever else you decide. This is different from leaving the gift outright because if any money was left over from an outright gift, it would go into the parent's estate, not yours.

If you want to make arrangements for someone other than your spouse or children, discuss this with your estate planner, who should be able to come up with some ideas for how to make it work to the best advantage of both the beneficiary and your estate.

In addition to your will, think about what would happen to these individuals if you were to become ill or incapacitated. Hopefully you will prepare an Enduring Power of Attorney which will allow someone to step in and take care of your finances, but the person you appoint (your "attorney") will not be able to give financial support to these other dependents unless your document specifically allows it.

Your Enduring Power of Attorney may always be used to look after your needs and those of your spouse and children without you having to request that. However, other dependents such as an aging parent do not fall within the usual parameters and you must specifically mention them if you want your Attorney to look after them.

CHAPTER 2: TAKING STOCK – ASSETS AND LIABILITIES

Before delving into the planning of your will and incapacity documents and deciding who gets what, you need to have a good understanding of what's in your estate. You need to know the type of asset, the way it is held, its value, and its likely tax treatment.

As you gain a better view of your finances, you will also get a better idea of exactly how you will be able to provide for the various beneficiaries in your family. When planning for children, in particular, this can affect your plans in terms of how the money will be held in trust. For example, if you were leaving your child a million dollars, you might want that inheritance to be handled differently than if it were a thousand dollars.

It's important to have a ballpark idea of how tax will affect your estate, which is largely a result of the type of asset you own. Sometimes a careful review of your assets makes it clear that there is not enough cash in the estate to pay tax without selling some property. Knowing this information in advance gives you the chance to take steps such as buying life insurance or changing the designation on a current life insurance policy in order to free up more cash. If that's not an option, you might wish to distribute your estate in a specific way, knowing that certain assets will have to be sold to pay the taxes. Having more information gives you a chance to make better, more realistic, decisions about how you will distribute your estate.

It's true that the value of your estate fluctuates over time. What you have today may not be what you have when you pass away. However, without a crystal ball, the best anyone can do is to plan according to what you have now. When making your will and your Enduring Power of Attorney, make the next five years your focus. Once you get beyond that time period, it becomes harder to predict what will happen. Children grow up and have children of their own. You marry, retire, or change jobs. Your needs change, and so does your financial picture. It is realistic to use your present situation as the basis for your planning because it is all that you know for sure. You might win a lottery or you might not. You might inherit money from your own parents or you might not. But what you know for sure is what is in place right now.

A. Real estate

Start by looking at real estate that you own. This will include:
- your home
- rental properties
- cabin or summer home
- raw land, and
- mines and minerals interests.

The estate planning process is a perfect time for you to check on any titles or properties that have been around for a long time, especially if they were passed down to you through your family. If you are not absolutely sure about whose names are on the title to a particular property or whether the property is jointly owned with someone else, this is a good time to find out. This can easily be done by going down to the local land titles registry and completing a search. This is very inexpensive. Most lawyers will do the search for you if you prefer.

The reason you want to know for sure whose name is on the title and how the property is held is that these facts affect your ability to dispose of the property in your will. For example, if you own a property jointly with your spouse, when one of you passes away the other one will take title to the whole property by right of survivorship. This means that you cannot leave the property to anyone else in your will if your spouse outlives you. You can't give away what you don't own outright.

However, if you own a property as tenants-in-common with another person, there is no right of survivorship. You would be able to leave your portion of the property to someone in your will. Obviously you cannot decide where your estate is going to go if you are not sure what you own, so checking on titles is a good first step.

Be sure to read chapter 5, which discusses joint property in more detail.

B. Digital assets

These days, most people have at least some digital assets, though they rarely think of them as assets, and not all estate lawyers will direct their clients to think about them. Millions of people have online profiles on social media programs such as Facebook, Instagram, Twitter, LinkedIn, and many others. Others have their own webpages and blogs. Many thousands keep their photographs online instead of in traditional albums, and have reward points from airline programs and shops. And some have online sources of income such as virtual shops, blogs, or vendor accounts on programs such as eBay or Etsy.

In addition, many Canadians use the internet to do their banking, investing, emailing, and shopping, as well as to read the news and flip through their favourite magazines. Many of those who make purchases online have a Paypal or other online payment account.

All of these are considered digital assets, even though not all of them have an ascertainable dollar value. As you think about your usage of the internet, you may conclude that you have more digital assets than you realized.

All of these profiles, accounts, and programs are protected by passwords so that you are the only one who can use them. This is designed to prevent fraud and identity theft and works well while you're alive, but it makes it impossible for anyone else to access your digital assets after you have passed away.

If your executor or your family members don't know your passwords for these various items, they will not be able to collect any funds that are sitting there in your name (such as a Paypal or eBay account) or to close your profiles on social media sites. These assets, like all assets belonging to someone who passes away, must be gathered in by the executor, added to the estate, and eventually paid out to the beneficiaries. An executor who does not collect the digital assets is just as liable for the loss as an executor who doesn't deal with a house or bank account.

However, digital assets can be very problematic for executors to deal with. Most of the social media sites have very strict rules that prevent them from providing access to another person's site, even when they are told that the person has passed away. To date, they have been remarkably uncooperative. Their policies – including their policy of not sharing your digital asset with anyone after you die - are set out in the fine print of the agreement made with each member who signs up, so it is very difficult to get around them. In some cases, it takes a lawsuit.

The solution to this problem is not one that is specifically addressed in a will. That would actually be a poor choice of a place to disclose your passwords for the simple reason that passwords change over time and if you tried to communicate them through your will, you would have to change your will many more times than you would find convenient. Also, wills become public documents once they are submitted for probate, so if they contained your passwords, they would become public knowledge.

The best way to deal with digital assets is to leave a comprehensive list of passwords, user names, and account numbers either for your executor or for a close family member. For obvious reasons, security is an issue because you want your list of passwords to be found after your death, but during your lifetime you don't want it lying around where anyone can come across it. If you have a safe at home, that would be a good choice of storage location, assuming that your executor would be able to gain access to the safe after you're gone.

A useful option is a workbook that gives you space to list not just your traditional assets, but your digital assets as well. These workbooks are practical even when you don't own digital assets, but are especially useful when you need a good place to record passwords. There are a few different ones on the market, so ensure that you get one that addresses digital assets.

Your executor would then sign on to your account or profile as if he or she were you, save documents or photos, allocate points to other accounts, collect financial assets into your bank account, and eventually delete the entire account or profile.

Some digital assets are less trouble than others. For example, even when a deceased has done the majority of his or her banking online, the executor of the estate can access the accounts by going into the bank branch and dealing in person with the staff there. Not every asset can be accessed this way. The best idea by far is to leave a list of your user names and passwords as well as a list of the sites you use, for your executor.

C. Bank accounts and investments

When planning your estate, make a detailed list of your liquid and almost-liquid assets including:
- Bank accounts in your name
- Bank accounts in joint names with others
- Investment portfolios (non-registered) in your name
- Investment portfolios (non-registered) in joint names with others
- Bank accounts that you have set up "in trust for" someone such as a child or grandchild

- Registered retirement savings plans (RRSP) or registered retirement income funds (RRIF) in your name
- Tax-free savings accounts (TFSA) in your name

When listing these accounts, make sure you understand the ownership of each account, whether you are the only owner or you own it jointly with another person. The ownership arrangement will affect how much control, if any, you will have over the account when you pass away.

If you own the account jointly with someone else (unless it is jointly owned between a parent and child or other intergenerational arrangement), and that person survives you, that person will own the account by right of survivorship. This means that you cannot give away the account in your will unless the other joint owner has already passed away before you. Be sure to read chapter 5 to learn more about inter-generational joint assets and how they affect your estate.

For registered accounts, make sure you know who you have named as the beneficiary of the asset. You may have to check with the bank if you cannot recall, especially if some of your assets have been in place for years. Your non-registered accounts and investments will not have a designated beneficiary as that is not possible on that type of account.

The beneficiary designation restricts your ability to deal with the asset because upon your death, the asset will be paid directly to the beneficiary you have named. It will not go into your estate. It won't be handled by your executor and it won't be covered by your will. An exception to this is if you name your estate as the beneficiary; in that case the asset will become part of your general estate and be handled under your will.

In addition, if you name someone as the beneficiary of an asset and that person dies before you, the asset goes into your estate, not theirs.

As you discuss your estate plan and make decisions about how you want to leave your estate after your death, you may decide that you want to change some of your beneficiary designations. For example, let's say that Lois, a widow, wants to leave $10,000 to each of her three grandchildren in her will. She reviews her assets, and sees that she has set things up as follows:
- Her life insurance has been left directly to her children;
- Her RRIF has been left directly to her children;
- Her TFSA has been left directly to her children;
- She has only a nominal amount of cash in her bank account, usually around $5,000, that she uses to run her household.

Though Lois has plenty of money and will have a large estate, she has nothing to leave her grandchildren in her will because all of her assets have designated beneficiaries. All of her assets will go straight to named beneficiaries without passing through her estate. Therefore if Lois wants to leave cash to her grandchildren, she needs to re-arrange some of her assets so that they become available. She could, for example, change the beneficiary designation on one of her assets so that it becomes payable to her estate rather than to her children. Or she could remove some funds from one of her other assets and place them into her bank account. If she chooses to do the latter, perhaps the amounts she is required to take out of her RRIF could be placed in the bank account.

This is an area in which Lois's financial advisor could be of great help to re-arrange her assets to attain her changing goals.

D. Pensions

When you pass away, if you have worked for wages in Canada, your estate is most likely eligible to receive a Canada Pension Plan death benefit after you pass away. Currently, the maximum amount available is $2,500.

Many Canadians are also eligible to receive pensions from government sources (such as Canada Pension Plan retirement benefits or Old Age Security benefits) or from private sources that are usually employers or previous employers. Sometimes there are also pensions available from other countries if an individual lived or worked in another country for a significant amount of time.

While pension plans vary from each other in many ways, there are some rules that they have in common. One such rule is that the pension plan will quite often state that if you have a spouse, that spouse is going to be the recipient of any remaining benefits of your plan after you pass away. This means that you will not be able to name a different beneficiary, such as your children, as long as you have a spouse who survives you.

In some cases you will be further restricted as to how you can deal with your pension due to a matrimonial property settlement. In most pension plans, once the plan owner dies, there is a reduced monthly benefit available to the spouse for a certain amount of time. Splitting a pension with a former spouse is often done as part of the division of assets when a couple gets divorced. Keep any such settlement in mind when planning what to do with your pension.

When you start your estate planning process, it is worthwhile to review the material that your pension plan administrator has provided to you so that you understand what benefits your plan (or plans) is going to provide after your death. Some plans have a lump sum death benefit available, but many others do not. Knowing how your pension plan works will help you determine exactly what position your spouse and other family members will be in after your passing, and what you have available to give them.

This is particularly important for an individual who is in a second marriage and who is trying to determine how to balance existing and future assets between the various parties he or she must look after.

E. Liabilities

While most people understand that making a will means they have to decide who is getting which assets, they often forget to take the effect of their debts into consideration. In some cases, an estate with millions of dollars in assets may end up with nothing left for beneficiaries simply because there are more debts than there are assets.

As you plan the distribution of your estate among your loved ones, make sure that you think about how your debts will affect your plans. Some of the most common debts that people forget to take into consideration are:
- Capital gains tax
- Income tax on registered instruments such as RRSPs and RRIFs
- Mortgages
- Credit card balances
- Car loans
- Lines of credit

As discussed in an earlier chapter, all of your debts and taxes must be paid before your beneficiaries may receive anything from your estate. Debts are paid from your general estate, which means they are borne equally by all residuary beneficiaries of your estate.

CHAPTER 3: DEFINING YOUR GOALS

To achieve your goals with your estate planning, you need to be clear on what those goals are. Not everyone wants the same thing, since every individual, every family, and every set of circumstances varies. There are some goals that are shared by many people, such as treating all of their kids equally under the will, and there are other goals, such as looking after an elderly parent, that are less frequent. Before seeing your lawyer, put some thought into what you really want to have happen after you're gone.

This is not to say that you must have all the answers before you go to see your lawyer. In fact, you should go in with an open mind, ready to hear suggestions and new information and ideas. However, if you know where, ultimately, you want your estate to go, your meeting will be shorter and the drafting and amending process will be much briefer. Ultimately, this will save you time and money and will ensure that you get the will you want.

Below, you'll see some examples of goals that are often expressed by people who are in the process of having their wills prepared. Each of these goals is followed by a few ideas of how those goals can be fine-tuned and achieved. You may find that some of these goals match your own. You may also find that looking over this list helps you define what you want for your own family. Keep in mind that you are not restricted to having only one goal in mind; it's certainly possible to have several, and your lawyer should be able to help you put all of them together into a workable plan.

A. Look after spouse

Looking after your spouse is one of the most common estate planning goals. In fact, when you review your assets, as you would have done in the previous chapter of this book, you most likely found that you had already set up some of your finances in a way that protects your spouse.

Canada Revenue Agency has rules in place that help couples look after each other financially when one of them passes away. For example, an individual can name his or her spouse as the beneficiary of an RRSP or RRIF, and when the individual dies, the RRSP or RRIF rolls over to the named spouse without any tax being payable at the time. This is an advantage that is not available when you name other beneficiaries (except, in limited circumstances, a disabled, dependent child).

A rollover to a spouse can also be used to transfer shares of a privately-owned business so that no capital gains tax is payable at the time they pass from the owner to his or her spouse. Again, this is a tax advantage designed to protect the couple. These are among the strategies you might consider as you work through your estate plan.

B. Equally among children

Many parents state that they want to treat all of their children equally when both parents have passed away. Though this is not required by law, it's such a widespread practice that many people believe it is the law.

You do not have to leave any part of your estate to your children who are adults and who are independent of you. They are not dependents in the legal sense of the word if they are not being supported by you financially on a regular basis. In Canada, only people who live in British Columbia can challenge their parents' wills on the basis that it is unfair to leave them out.

If you have decided to treat all of your children equally, you might be surprised to find how easily that seemingly simple directive can be thwarted by other steps you have already taken. For example, let's say that you have a life insurance policy for $100,000 that names all three of your children as beneficiaries. The rest of your estate is worth $200,000. You have a will that says that your estate is to be divided among all of your children equally. So far, so good. But let's say that one of your children passes away before you do. Your will says that in such case, your child's children receive your deceased child's share. So your estate is still divided into thirds. Each of your children gets $66,666. The final third is divided among your deceased child's kids. But what about your life insurance? It does not get divided three ways; it is split between the two surviving children, who each get $50,000 from the insurance.

The end result is:

Child A	$116,666
Child B	$116,666
Child C	$66,666 Paid to his children

As you can see, the goal of achieving equality among the children was not achieved because of the direct beneficiary designation on the life insurance policy.

Another very common example of trying – and failing – to leave an equal distribution among children involves the fact that some assets are taxable and some are not. Often, parents divide up the assets in a way that they think is going to result in their children receiving equal amounts but forget to factor in the taxes.

As an example, let's look at a situation in which Ali wants to leave equal amounts to his three children. He has a home worth $250,000, a cabin worth $250,000, and about $250,000 in a bank account. He decides that his oldest child gets the home, the middle child gets the cabin, and the youngest gets the account. He thinks he has treated them all equally, but he has not.

The oldest child will receive the house worth $250,000 and there is no tax impact on anyone because it is Ali's principal residence. The middle child will receive the cabin worth $250,000, but the capital gains tax on the cabin is $50,000. That is not paid by the middle child, but comes out of Ali's general estate; in other words it comes out of the bank account. The youngest child is supposed to get $250,000 as well, but actually will only get what is in the account once the tax on the cabin ($50,000) as well as expenses such as the funeral have been paid. This is not how Ali wanted his estate to go because it does not reach his goal of treating the children equally, but it happens this way because Ali neglected to consider how the tax would be paid.

C. Equal vs fair

The main reason that parents want to treat their children equally is that they believe this is the way to be fair to all of the children. However, equal is not always the same as fair.

In some cases, one of the children has done something to increase the value of the parents' estate that the other children have not done. Perhaps the child has farmed the parents' land or has helped run the family business. Or maybe the child has lived nearby and has helped the parents by painting the house or building the fence. To some parents, this means that the child who has helped more should receive more than the other children, who have done less to build up or preserve what the parents have to give to the kids.

In other cases, the parent might already have helped one child more than the others, such as by giving one child funds to make a down payment on a home without giving the same to the other children.

In situations like this, the parents might conclude that it would actually be more fair if the children were treated unequally. Perhaps the daughter who has been running the family business and successfully doubling the profits for the parents should receive more than the other children who have moved away and pursued their own careers. Maybe the child who received a large down payment should receive less than the others because he has already had some help from the parents. While there is no right or wrong answer for everyone on this issue, it is worthwhile for parents to consider whether an equal distribution among the children really is the fair way to go.

If you are making a will in which you are leaving different amounts to your children and you are doing this because you believe it is the way to treat all of your children fairly, consider making a statement in your will that briefly explains why you are doing so. This can go a long way to preventing hurt feelings, misunderstandings, accusations, and lawsuits. For example, instead of making a will in which you say that your son, Tom, is to receive $30,000 less than his siblings without any explanation, consider saying something in the will such as:

> *"I love all of my children equally but I am making an unequal distribution among them in this will because I have helped one more than the others during my lifetime"*.

A simple statement such as that would explain to Tom that he was not actually punished or left out.

D. Advances to your children

During their lifetimes, parents frequently help out one or more of their adult children financially. They'll sometimes give the child a sum of money for a down payment on a home or to buy a vehicle. Though it generally does not occur to anyone at the time, this is an action that causes a surprisingly large number of estate fights.

The problem is not with the idea advancing funds, as parents have every right to do so. Neither is the problem with the children who accept the money. The problem is that the law surrounding the giving or lending of money to the children is simply not well known, so it is rarely dealt with properly before the death of the parents.

The law says that when a parent gives or lends a significant sum of money to an adult child, the money is an advance on the child's inheritance. Because it's an advance, the child must repay it before receiving his or her share of the parent's estate. This is what some parents want, but not necessarily what all parents want. Some are adamant that the money they gave their child was a gift, and they have told the child that it does not have to be repaid. Many are shocked during the estate planning process when they find out that their generosity could lead to serious disputes, even if nobody is being greedy.

The problem arises when the parent passes away and the children begin dealing with the estate. All of a sudden, the executor is told by the estate lawyer that advances to the children must be repaid. This is always a huge problem. For one thing, the transaction is almost never recorded, so there is confusion about what was given and what, if anything, was repaid. Secondly, the child who received the money and was told by the parents that it was a gift is angry at being told it's coming out of his or her inheritance. The child was told by the parents that it need not be repaid. This often becomes a personal dispute between that child and the executor because the child sees it as being unfair. The child usually accuses the executor of being wrong, or biased against him or her.

Finally, the problem is exacerbated because the law does not set out a dollar value for what is significant and what is not. This leads to disputes among the kids about who received what and whether those amounts should be repaid.

The problem is further aggravated by the fact that the executor of the estate does not have the legal authority to choose to ignore the advance. Doing so creates a loss to the estate and the executor is personally liable for repaying such losses. So a sibling acting as an executor cannot simply look the other way without the risk of being sued by the remaining beneficiaries.

This scenario is more common than people realize. If you have lent or given money to one or more of your adult children, it is essential that you address the situation in your will. If you want the advances to be repaid, confirm this in your will. This will back up your executor so that your children will know that he or she is simply doing the job and not being greedy.

If you don't want any advances to be repaid, then you must address this in your will. If you do not specifically say that you don't want the money repaid or set off, your executor will have no choice in the matter and will have to reduce the child's inheritance by the amount of money you have given the child.

E. Balance a blended family

Estate planning for those who have married (or entered a common law relationship) more than once and have children from a previous relationship can truly be a balancing act. This is because they are bound by a number of legal obligations that restrict the goals they can set. In other words, there are dependents who must be supported in a will and a person with a blended family may well have a number of dependents with competing claims.

For example, an individual who has married for the second time might have a spouse who must, by law, receive some part of the estate, as well as minor children from the previous marriage who must receive some part of the estate. In addition, the same individual might have adult children from the previous marriage who, though they are not financial dependents, may have a moral right to some part of the estate in the eyes of the parent. This can make for somewhat tricky planning, but it can certainly be done with careful consideration and discussion.

When deciding which assets should go to which beneficiaries, think about whether one path offers more tax benefits than another. For example, if you were thinking of leaving some cash to your new spouse, as well as some cash to your children of the previous marriage, the source of those funds can make a difference to your estate. Let's say that you have an RRSP worth $50,000 and a bank account worth $50,000. There are two ways this could play out:

First scenario:

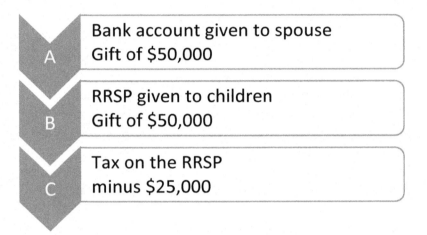

A — Bank account given to spouse
Gift of $50,000

B — RRSP given to children
Gift of $50,000

C — Tax on the RRSP
minus $25,000

$75,000   **total gift to family members**

Here is the second possible scenario using the same assets but switching around who receives them:

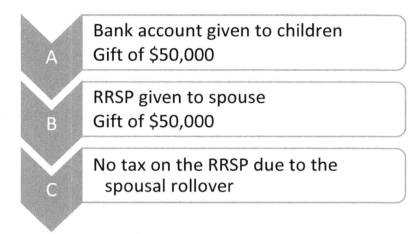

- **A**: Bank account given to children — Gift of $50,000
- **B**: RRSP given to spouse — Gift of $50,000
- **C**: No tax on the RRSP due to the spousal rollover

$100,000   total gift to family members

By strategically allocating your assets, you have made the most of the money you have available in your estate and minimized the amount payable in taxes. This is a simple example, of course, and in some estates assets can be very complex, but it illustrates the point that you should put some thought into how your assets are distributed.

F. Leave a legacy

Many thousands of Canadians have included gifts to charitable organizations in their wills. Unfortunately, not all of those gifts will find their way to the intended recipients. Some will be the subject of court disputes due to mistakes in the wills.

If you want to make a charitable gift in your will, you must be very clear and very specific about exactly who is supposed to receive that gift. For example, it is not enough to say you want to leave a donation to "cancer" or to "homeless animals". Each of those topics will turn up dozens of hits if searched, and each of those hits represents a group or organization that would like to receive your gift. Keep in mind that you won't be around to clarify any confusion, so you must be specific in your will. Instead of saying that you want to make a donation to "cancer", describe which hospital or foundation or organization you want to benefit, and include the address as well.

If you are not specific, each of the dozens of possible candidates may decide to try to be confirmed as the recipient of the gift, which means a lawsuit. Your estate will end up paying legal fees to clarify your gift, which will reduce either the gift to the charity itself or the gift to your other beneficiaries. If your executor pays the gift to one beneficiary and then the court decides that someone else is the right beneficiary, your executor may be sued personally for the amount of the gift. The easiest way to confirm the proper name, address, and charitable registration number for the group you want to benefit is to go to the charitable organization database that is maintained by Canada Revenue Agency. It is online and there is no cost to use it.

When you make a charitable donation in your will, you have the option to state the purpose for which you want your gift to be used. Stating a specific purpose works better in some situations than in others, so it is a good idea to ask a few questions before settling on a purpose. For example, you might wish to leave a monetary gift to your church. If you said that you wanted your gift to be added to the building fund for the new steeple, your gift can only be used for that purpose. If the church doesn't have a building fund for a new steeple, your gift is going to be a problem rather than a gift. However, if you simply say that it is to go to the church and you don't mention the steeple fund, it will be used for whatever purpose the church deems most urgent or most suitable.

This is not to say that you can never specify a purpose, only that you should be careful to confirm that your choice is an appropriate one. If your will was made many years ago, this is something that you might have to update, as the needs and goals of any given organization may change from time to time.

If you want to make a gift to a hospital, foundation, or university, be aware that those institutions employ staff whose job it is to work with potential donors to ensure that the gift in the will is properly worded and that the gift ultimately makes it to your chosen destination. You can access those charitable planners at no cost, and this is a great way to find out more about how your gift might be used by the institution.

When your lawyer drafts your will to include a charitable donation, he or she should also include clauses to help ensure that unforeseen circumstances don't interfere with your gift. Over time, charitable organizations may stop operating, or be amalgamated into other charities with similar purposes. You don't want those changes to prevent your gift from being carried out if you can possibly avoid that.

For example, your will might leave a gift in your will to an animal shelter on Main Street. A few years after your make your will, the shelter on Main Street closes its doors forever, but it merges with a larger, newer shelter on First Street to share resources and better serve its purposes. If your gift is directed specifically to the Main Street shelter, it is no longer possible for your gift to be carried out because the shelter no longer exists. However, if your will says that gifts can be made to successor charitable organizations, then the gift can be made to the shelter on First Street.

Another very useful clause for your will is one that gives your executor the ability to choose another charitable organization with goals as similar as possible to the one you had named, if the one you named no longer exists. These additional clauses for your will are something you should discuss with your lawyer at the time you plan your charitable giving.

G. Keep land in the family

Quite often, individuals want to ensure that certain parcels of land are kept within the family in future generations. In many cases this is due to the fact that the land was first bought by or granted to ancestors and the individual wants to carry on that tradition. In other cases the land in question is a cabin or summer house that is new to the family but has been a source of great family experiences and memories.

While keeping land within the family is certainly an understandable goal, it has to be done very carefully in order to avoid arguments and legal tangles.

The first issue that crops up is exactly who is meant by "family" when the goal is to keep it in the family. Usually parents want to hand the property down to the next generation, so the word "family" really refers to their children. This is a good starting point but unfortunately that's usually the limit in terms of the thought process for parents. They decide to put all of the children's names on the cabin so that all of the children will own the cabin equally.

This is an absolutely terrible idea that in almost every case results in an ugly dispute among the children.

What parents fail to appreciate is that each of their children has or will one day have his or her own spouse and children. Instead of one family wishing to use the cabin, there will be a number of families all wanting to use the same cabin, generally at the same time. Working out who is going to use the cabin on any given weekend is extremely difficult when the parents are no longer alive to control the situation.

Parents also forget that when there are several owners of a property, all of those owners have to agree on matters such as whether the roof needs to be repaired, whether a well needs to be dug, whether the place can be rented out, and if so to whom and for how much.

The children who use the cabin infrequently may not think it's fair that they have to pay an equal share of property tax and maintenance when they rarely use the cabin and others use it all the time. If they refuse to pay their share or don't have the financial wherewithal to do so, it ends up as a dispute with the other children.

Parents also don't appreciate that their kids may do things that are unexpected. For example, one of the kids may lose his or her home to foreclosure or divorce and decide to live in the cabin for a while, preventing others from using the cabin. Or one of the kids might have a friend who needs a place to go and lend or rent the cabin to that friend. If one of the children makes these arrangements by himself or herself without the agreement of the others (which happens frequently) then again, there is a dispute.

If things get so bad that the children decide to sell the cabin, they are still likely to be locked into disputes over such items as the selling price, the closing date, whether renovations need to be done first, whether the contents of the cabin are included, and the wishes of any of them that wants to buy out the others.

In other words, putting everyone's name on the cabin doesn't work. It is a fact proven multiple times that it does not work. Parents need to put more effort and creativity into deciding what to do with the cabin and not leave a giant legal mess for the children to deal with.

If you have a cabin or home that you want to keep in the family, start by having frank conversations with your children about their wishes. Find out who is interested in owning it and who isn't. Don't assume that all of the children want to own the property. Your discussions with them will probably reveal the fact that one or more of them would rather buy their own cabin, or use their in-laws' cabin, or is simply not particularly interested.

Once you have a better idea of who in the family might be the recipient of the cabin, start thinking about how it might be accomplished. You may wish to have a conversation with your estate planning lawyer to get ideas that are tailored to your situation, and the following paragraphs contain some ideas that you might pursue.

Think about the value of the cabin. How does the value compare to the size of each child's inheritance? If the cabin's value is small compared to the child's overall inheritance, you might want to say in your will that the child may have the cabin as part of his or her share of your estate.

If the cabin is worth more than what the child is going to inherit from you, you might consider including in your will an option for a child to purchase the cabin from your estate using his or her inheritance as the down payment.

For example, let's say that each of your four children is going to inherit about $100,000 from you. Your cabin is worth $150,000 and you would like your son John to have the cabin. Your will could say that John has the option to buy the cabin, using up to $100,000 from your estate, so he would only have to come up with $50,000 from his own resources.

If you have more than one child who expresses an interest in the cabin, you might say that John has 60 days (or some other number of days) to exercise his option to buy the cabin, and if he doesn't do so within that time, another one of your children has the same option. This gives some structure for the executor of the estate to follow when dealing with the cabin.

When leaving a cabin, summer home, raw land, or rental properties in your estate, remember that they are subject to capital gains tax (more about that in chapter 7) and that the tax is not paid by the person who receives the property. The tax is paid by the entire estate, unless your will says otherwise.

For example, let's say that when your cabin transfers from you to John, there is a capital gains tax bill of $40,000. Many parents mistakenly believe that the tax goes with the property and therefore don't even address the taxes, but the tax bill comes out of the estate before the kids get their shares. Here is how it would actually look:

Estate value before tax: $400,000
John's share before tax: $100,000
Joe's share before tax: $100,000
Jane's share before tax: $100,000
Jill's share before tax: $100,000

The cabin transfers to John, then:
Estate value less tax: (400,000 – 40,000 = 360,000)

John's share after tax: Cabin less his contribution from his own resources and less his ¼ of the capital gains tax
(150,000 – 50,000 – 10,000)
John: $90,000
Joe: $90,000
Jane: $90,000
Jill: $90,000

As you can see, John gets the cabin, but all of the children share the tax on the cabin equally. Though this is the correct procedure, it can be a source of real resentment by the children who do not receive the cabin. Often it results in accusations of favoritism or fraud against the executor. Quite often it looks to the other children in the family that the executor is either simply making a big mistake, or is deliberately favouring one beneficiary. To avoid that kind of dispute, if you are going to include an option to purchase, consider also including a clause saying that the person who takes the cabin also takes the tax on the cabin.

A similar clause can be used to address any asset that is going to incur capital gains tax or income tax.

H. Hand down the family business

A lot of owners of small businesses say that they are so busy running their business and trying to make it profitable that they don't really have time to think about what's going to happen when they retire, lose mental capacity, or pass away. However, it's essential to have some plans in place for those eventualities. Otherwise, if you pass away unexpectedly or are sidelined by a stroke or heart attack, your business affairs may be left hanging with nobody authorized to carry them on in your place.

As this chapter is about setting goals and not about the logistics of the transaction, at this point you should direct your mind to what you would like to see happen with your business, as opposed to how to achieve the goal. In other words, you need to think about what you want for yourself, your business, and others involved in the business. In some cases, the future of the company has already been decided by way of a shareholders' agreement that provides for the purchase of your shares by the other owners of the company.

But what if you are the only owner of the business, or you and your spouse own it together? You should be thinking about where that business is going to go one day in the future.

Is it your wish that the business be taken over by one or more of your children? A mistake that some business owners make is assuming that the children want to take over the business, without ever actually asking them what they want. Before deciding that one of your children would be a perfect CEO for your business, have a frank discussion about their wishes and plans. Even those of your children who currently help out in the business may not wish to make running the business their future career.

Assuming that you have spoken with the kids and one of them is going to follow you into the business and eventually own it, you must take the appropriate steps to make that happen. There are a few options to consider, depending on your circumstances and your wishes.

As part of your goal-setting for your business, think about whether you would like to sell it, receive the funds in a bulk payment that you can invest, or whether you'd rather receive income from the company for a number of years into the future. The difference here could mean a direct sale either to the children or a third party as opposed to an estate freeze that would allow your purchaser to redeem your shares for income over time.

Rolled into that question is the issue of how you would like to be involved in the company after you sell it. Will you sever all ties and let them simply carry on in their own way? Or will you continue to lend your expertise as a consultant? Understanding your goal for continued involvement – or not- may help you decide whether a sale or a freeze is a better option for you. If you are going to continue to be involved in the company, you will have some input into the future financial health of the company, which may make you feel safer in terms of relying on the company for your future income.

I. **Intestacy**

If you pass away without a valid will in place, you are said to have died "intestate". Every province and territory in Canada has its own laws that set out who gets what when someone dies intestate, and they vary quite a bit across the country. You may be surprised at how your estate would be distributed if you were to die without having put your plans in place. Many individuals simply assume that their spouses will inherit everything, though that is simply not the case. The rights of a spouse depend on the size of the estate, whether there are children, the number of children, the existence of a pre-nuptial agreement, joint property arrangements, beneficiary designations, and of course whether the marriage is legal or common law.

If you die without a will, others will have to make decisions for you. Without a will, you won't have an executor in place. Therefore, someone will have to come forward and apply to the court to be the administrator of your estate, and it might not be a person that you would have chosen.

In some cases, nobody comes forward because they don't want the trouble of dealing with the family, or because they fear they might somehow become liable for the deceased's debts. In some cases, the government (in the form of the Office of the Public Trustee) will assume the responsibility for administering the estate. In other words, you will have absolutely no say in who looks after your estate if you don't have a will.

Without a will, you'll also lose the chance to make arrangements that deal with the distribution of your estate. For example, if your children are going to inherit from you, they will receive their whole share as soon as they become adults and you will have lost the chance to set up trusts that could protect their inheritance. You won't be able to leave anything to your favourite charity, or to close friends and relatives. The law will decide for you where your estate is going to go.

Below is a table that summarizes what will happen to your estate if you die without a will. You will note that in most parts of Canada, your spouse will receive what is known as a "spousal preferred share", which means that your spouse will be first in line to receive something from your estate, though it is not the entire estate. There is generally a dollar amount placed on that share, and anything above that dollar amount is split between your spouse and other beneficiaries.

It's important to understand what exactly is included in your estate in a discussion about how your estate will be distributed on intestacy. This discussion refers to your assets that are in your name. It does *not* include the following assets:

- Any assets held in joint names when the other joint owner is still alive (subject to the discussion above about inter-generational joint ownership); or
- Any assets that directly name a beneficiary that is not your estate, when that beneficiary is still alive.

Table 2: *Distribution of an estate on intestacy according to province or territory*

Province or territory	Distribution of estate when there is no will
Alberta	Where there is a spouse or adult interdependent partner (AIP) but no children, all to the spouse or AIP.

Where there is a spouse or AIP and one or more children, the whole estate goes to the spouse or AIP if all of the children of the deceased are also the children of the spouse or AIP.

Where there is a spouse or AIP and at least one child is not the child of the spouse or AIP, the spouse or AIP gets the greater of $150,000 or 50% of the net value of the estate. The rest of the estate is divided among the children.

If there is both a spouse and an AIP as well as children, half of the amount described above goes to the spouse and the other half goes to the AIP, with the rest going to the children.

If there is a spouse and an AIP but no children, half the estate goes to the |

	spouse and half goes to the AIP. If the deceased and his/her spouse were separated and had either a) lived apart for 2 years, or b) signed a separation agreement, then the spouse is does not get anything. Where there is no spouse or AIP, the estate is divided equally among the deceased's children. If a child has predeceased, that deceased child's share is divided among his or her children. Where the deceased leaves no spouse, AIP, children or grandchildren, the estate goes to his or her parents. If the parents are not alive, then to the deceased's siblings (including half-siblings). If there are no siblings alive, then to the deceased's grandparents. If the grandparents are not alive, then to the descendants of the grandparents.
British Columbia	Where there is a spouse but no children, the estate all goes to the spouse. If there is a spouse as well as descendants (children or grandchildren), the spouse gets all of the household furnishings and goods,

as well as a preferential share. The amount of the preferential share is not always the same. If all of the deceased's children are also children of the surviving spouse, then the spouse's preferential share is $300,000. If one or more of the deceased's children are not the spouse's child, then the spouse's preferential share is $150,000. After that, the remainder of the estate is split so that half goes to the spouse and half is divided among all of the children.

If the deceased had both a married spouse and a common law spouse, they have to divide the spouse's share between them.

If there is no spouse, the estate is divided among the deceased's children. If one of the deceased's children has already passed away, the deceased child's share will be divided equally among the deceased child's children (grandchildren of the deceased).

If the deceased left no children or grandchildren, the estate goes to his or her parents.

If the parents are not alive, the estate is divided among the deceased's siblings (including half siblings).

If there are no siblings alive, then the estate goes to the deceased's

	grandparents.
Manitoba	Where there is a spouse or a common law partner but no children, all to the spouse or common law partner.

Where there is a spouse or common law partner as well as children, and all of the children of the deceased are also the children of the spouse or common law partner, the entire estate goes to the spouse or common law partner.

Where there is a spouse or common law partner and at least one child who is not the child of the spouse or common law partner, the spouse or common law partner will get the greater of $50,000 or one half of the estate. The rest will be divided among the children.

A married spouse who was separated from the deceased does not get anything from the estate if he or she or the deceased had filed for divorce, if one of them had applied to the court for equalization of assets, if there had already been an equalization of assets, or if they had already divided their property between them.

A common law spouse who was separated from the deceased does not get anything if they had a registered relationship which they formally dissolved at the registry, if 3 years have passed since they separated, if one of |

them had applied to the court for an equalization of assets, or if they had already divided their property between them.

If the deceased had both a spouse and a common law partner, the most recent relationship is the one that is considered current.

Where there are children, but no spouse or common law partner, the estate is divided equally among the children. If a child has predeceased, that child's children receive the share of the deceased child.

Where there is no spouse, common law spouse, children, grandchildren or great-grandchildren, the estate goes to the deceased's parents.

If there are no parents alive, half goes to the maternal grandparents and half to the paternal grandparents. If both grandparents on one side have deceased, the share is divided among the grandparents' issue (children, grandchildren and/or great-grandchildren).

| New Brunswick | Where there is a spouse but no children, all to the spouse.

Where there is a spouse and one child, the spouse will receive the marital property, as well as one half of the estate, with the rest of the estate going to the child.

Where there is a spouse and more than one child, the spouse will receive the marital property as well as one third of the estate, with the rest of the estate being divided equally among the children.

If a child predeceases his or her parent, when the parent dies, the child's share goes to the child's living children or grandchildren, if any.

Where there is no spouse, children, grandchildren or great-grandchildren, the estate goes to the deceased person's parents.

If the parents are not alive, then the estate goes to the deceased's siblings, with the share of any deceased sibling going to the children of the deceased sibling.

If no siblings are then alive, the estate is divided among all nieces and nephews. |
|---|---|

Newfoundland & Labrador	Where there is a spouse but no children, all to the spouse.

Where there is a spouse and one child, half to the spouse and half to the child, regardless of the age of the child.

Where there is a spouse and more than one child, one third goes to the spouse and the rest divided equally among the children. If one of the children has died, then the child's children take the deceased child's share.

Nothing to common law spouses.

Where there is no spouse, children, or grandchildren, all to the deceased's parents. If no parents are alive, then all to the deceased's siblings. If one of the siblings has died, then the deceased sibling's children (nieces and nephews) take the deceased sibling's share. |
| Northwest Territories | Where there is a spouse and no children, the spouse receives the whole estate.

Where there is a spouse and children, the spouse gets the first $50,000 of the estate. The spouse may elect to receive the family home instead of the $50,000 if the home is worth more than $50,000.

If there is a spouse and one child, the spouse gets half of the rest of the estate, and the child gets the other |

half.

Where there is a spouse and more than one child, the spouse gets 1/3 and the children equally split the other 2/3.

If a child of the deceased died while the parent was still alive, and that deceased child left children of his or her own, the deceased child's children receive the share of the parent's estate that the deceased child would have received if living.

Where there are no spouse, children, or grandchildren, the estate goes to the parents of the deceased.

If the parents are not alive, the estate of the deceased is split equally among his or her siblings. If a sibling has predeceased, then the children of the deceased sibling receive the share that the deceased sibling would have received if living.

If none of those people are alive when the deceased passes away, the estate will be distributed equally to the people who are his or her next of kin.

Nova Scotia	Where there is a spouse and no children, the spouse receives the whole estate.
	Where there is a spouse and children, the spouse gets the first $50,000 of the estate. The spouse may elect to receive the family home instead of the $50,000 if the home is worth more than $50,000.
	If there is a spouse and one child, the spouse gets half of the rest of the estate, and the child gets the other half.
	Where there is a spouse and more than one child, the spouse gets 1/3 and the children equally split the other 2/3.
	If a child of the deceased died while the parent was still alive, and that deceased child left children of his or her own, the deceased child's children receive the share of the parent's estate that the deceased child would have received if living.
	Where there are no spouse, children, or grandchildren, the estate goes to the parents of the deceased.
	If the parents are not alive, the estate of the deceased is split equally among his or her siblings. If a sibling has predeceased, then the children of the deceased sibling receive the share that

	the deceased sibling would have received if living.

If none of those people are alive when the deceased passes away, the estate will be distributed equally to the people who are his or her next of kin. |
| Nunavut | Where there is a spouse and no children, the spouse receives the whole estate.

Where there is a spouse and children, the spouse gets the first $50,000 of the estate. The spouse may elect to receive the family home instead of the $50,000 if the home is worth more than $50,000.

If there is a spouse and one child, the spouse gets half of the rest of the estate, and the child gets the other half.

Where there is a spouse and more than one child, the spouse gets 1/3 and the children equally split the other 2/3.

If a child of the deceased died while the parent was still alive, and that deceased child left children of his or her own, the deceased child's children receive the share of the parent's estate that the deceased child would have received if living.

Where there are no spouse, children, or grandchildren, the estate goes to the |

	parents of the deceased.

If the parents are not alive, the estate of the deceased is split equally among his or her siblings. If a sibling has predeceased, then the children of the deceased sibling receive the share that the deceased sibling would have received if living.

If none of those people are alive when the deceased passes away, the estate will be distributed equally to the people who are his or her next of kin. |
| Ontario | Where there is a spouse but no children, all to the spouse.

Where there is a spouse and children, the spouse gets the first $200,000 of the estate.

Where there is partial intestacy and the will leaves the spouse less than $200,000, the spouse is entitled to receive that amount from the intestate assets.

Where there is a spouse and 1 child, after the first $200,000, the spouse gets ½ the estate and the child gets the other ½.

Where there is a spouse and more than 1 child, after the first $200,000, the spouse gets 1/3 of the estate and the rest is divided equally among the children. If any child of the deceased |

	died before the deceased, the share the deceased child would have received if living is divided among his or her children.
	Where there are no spouse, children or grandchildren, the estate will go to the parents of the deceased.
	If the parents are not alive, the estate of the deceased is split equally among his or her siblings. If a sibling has predeceased, then the children of the deceased sibling receive the share that the deceased sibling would have received if living.
	If none of those people are alive when the deceased passes away, the estate will be distributed equally to the people who are his or her next of kin.
Prince Edward Island	Where there is a spouse and no issue, all to the spouse.
	Where there is a spouse and one child, ½ of the estate goes to the spouse and the other ½ to the child.
	Where there is a spouse and more than one child, 1/3 goes to the spouse and the rest is divided equally among the children.
	If any child of the deceased died before the deceased, the share the deceased child would have received if living is divided among his or her children.

	Where there are no spouse, children or grandchildren, the estate will go to the parents of the deceased.

If the parents are not alive, the estate of the deceased is split equally among his or her siblings. If a sibling has predeceased, then the children of the deceased sibling receive the share that the deceased sibling would have received if living.

If none of those people are alive when the deceased passes away, the estate will be distributed equally to the people who are his or her next of kin. |
| Quebec | If there is no spouse and no children, the estate is divided among the deceased's parents, the deceased's siblings, and their descendants.

If there is a spouse but no children, the spouse gets 2/3 of the estate and the deceased's parents get 1/3.

If there is a spouse and children, and all of the children belong to both the deceased and the spouse, the spouse gets 1/3 and the children share 2/3.

If there is a spouse and children, and the children are from the deceased's previous marriage, the spouse gets 1/3 and the children share 2/3.

If there is no spouse but there are |

	children, all of the estate goes to the issue (children and, if a child is deceased, the grandchildren).

If there is a married spouse and a common law partner, the common law partner does not inherit. |
| Saskatchewan | Where there is a spouse but no children, all to the spouse.

Where there is a spouse and children, the spouse receives the first $100,000 of the estate.

Where there is a spouse and 1 child, after the first $100,000, the spouse gets ½ the estate and the child gets the other ½.

Where there is a spouse and more than 1 child, after the first $100,000, the spouse gets 1/3 of the estate and the rest is divided equally among the children. If any child of the deceased died before the deceased, the share the deceased child would have received if living is divided among his or her children.

Where there are no spouse, children or grandchildren, the estate will go to the parents of the deceased.

If the parents are not alive, the estate of the deceased is split equally among his or her siblings. If a sibling has predeceased, then the children of the |

	deceased sibling receive the share that the deceased sibling would have received if living.

If none of those people are alive when the deceased passes away, the estate will be distributed equally to the people who are his or her next of kin. |
| Yukon | Where there is a spouse but no children, all to the spouse.

Where there is a spouse and children, the spouse receives the first $75,000 of the estate.

Where there is a spouse and 1 child, after the first $75,000, the spouse gets ½ the estate and the child gets the other ½.

Where there is a spouse and more than 1 child, after the first $75,000, the spouse gets 1/3 of the estate and the rest is divided equally among the children. If any child of the deceased died before the deceased, the share the deceased child would have received if living is divided among his or her children.

Where there are no spouse, children or grandchildren, the estate will go to the parents of the deceased.

If the parents are not alive, the estate of the deceased is split equally among his or her siblings. If a sibling has |

| | predeceased, then the children of the deceased sibling receive the share that the deceased sibling would have received if living.

If none of those people are alive when the deceased passes away, the estate will be distributed equally to the people who are his or her next of kin. |

CHAPTER 4: ESTATE DOCUMENTS

In this chapter, we are going to take a look at the group of documents that usually makes up a person's estate plan. The vast majority of people need only three documents, those being a will, an Enduring Power of Attorney (sometimes known as a Continuing Power of Attorney or Power of Attorney for Property), and a health care directive (also known as a Personal Directive or Power of Attorney for Personal Care). Depending on the person's circumstances, they may need one or more of the other documents described in this chapter. By the time you have read this chapter, you should have at least a basic idea of whether those other documents would be helpful to you, and will recognize them if they are mentioned to you by your estate planning lawyer.

By becoming familiar with the purpose and scope of each of these documents, you will gain a good idea of what you need to shop for. Many consumers like to call around to various law firms to ask the price and have an initial chat before they make an appointment, so this chapter will help you understand what you need to ask about. Knowing the purpose of the documents will also help you make the most of your time with the lawyer as you will already be familiar with some of the subject matter.

If, when reading the description of these documents here, you aren't really sure if you need the documents, why not bring it up with your lawyer? That way you can get a legal opinion from someone who knows your specific circumstances and can advise you of whether a certain document would be helpful for you. Remember that a lawyer with experience in estate planning should be able to give you some ideas and suggestions for your planning that you may not have thought of on your own.

A. Will

A will is a document that directs where you want your assets to go after you have passed away. Though that is a simple concept, in reality it can be extremely complex, depending on the family situation and the extent and type of assets.

There are certain elements that must be present in every will in order for it to be effective. The first of those elements is the naming of an executor. This is the person who is in charge of the estate when the testator (the person whose will it is) has passed away. The executor is responsible for funeral arrangements, notifying beneficiaries, determining and locating assets, paying bills, preparing tax returns, sending the will to probate, and paying out the estate to the proper beneficiaries. That is an abbreviated list, of course, since there are dozens and dozens of other jobs that the executor must do as well.

Later in this chapter you will find a section about choosing your representatives, which will include several tips for deciding who should be your executor.

A will must deal with all of the assets of an estate. Often when people make their own wills without legal advice, they list each asset (house, bank account, car, etc.) and then name a beneficiary for each one. While this may be effective as far as it goes, it is not legally a complete will. There will always be some small item that is not listed, even if it is simply the furniture or used clothing. Wills must always include a clause that deals with the residue, or rest, of the estate, even when you think you've listed everything.

If a will doesn't contain a clause that gives away the residue, legally it creates a partial intestacy, which means the law says your will does not cover your whole estate. This opens up legal questions that are inconvenient to your survivors and may end up costing a lot more money than you saved by doing the will yourself.

The will must direct to whom your assets are to be given once all of the debts and expenses have been paid. The people who receive the estate are called beneficiaries. There are two main types of beneficiaries, those being the people sharing the residue or bulk of the estate ("residuary" beneficiaries), and those who are receiving only a specific item such as a piece of jewelry or a specified sum of money ("non-residuary" or "specific" beneficiaries).

There are requirements for signing and witnessing a will. Though the wording changes slightly from province to province, the requirements are largely the same. The testator must sign his or her will in front of two witnesses. He or she must also initial the bottom of each page in front of those witnesses. Then, each of the witnesses must sign in front of the testator and each other, and initial each page. If this procedure is not followed, the will is not properly executed and is not valid.

The witnesses can be anybody who has reached the age of majority and is mentally competent, but cannot be a beneficiary under the will or the spouse (legal or common law) of a beneficiary of the will.

You will find more ideas about how to create a really solid will in chapter 8 of this book. That chapter covers several suggestions for clauses that address specific concerns or situations and that will make your estate administration flow more smoothly. Note that all wills must be written down. No jurisdiction in Canada presently allows for videotaped or audiotaped wills.

The rules for signing and witnessing are different for holographic, or hand-written, wills and you will find a section of this chapter specifically about holographic wills below.

The person you name in your will to look after your estate is your executor. For many reasons, people often make a poor choice of executor. This happens with dismaying regularity, particularly with parents choosing unsuitable children to fill the role. Usually the reason is that they do not want to offend anyone by not choosing them. The end result is quite often an executor who lacks the skills or temperament to do the job and cannot get along with the rest of the family. This leads to arguments, speculation about what the executor is doing, delays, extra costs, and ultimately the loss of family relationships.

Another common mistake made by parents is naming all of the children together as executors. Again, this springs from the fact that parents don't want to appear to be favouring one child over another. It ends up with nobody actually being in charge because everyone must do every single thing together. Realistically, complete cooperation rarely happens with siblings because they have different personalities and values. They also have childhood resentments and issues that are brought back up by the loss of a parent. Naming all of the children together is a notoriously bad idea.

Some of the characteristics of an ideal executor are:
- Someone who is younger than you, or at least no older than you are
- Honest and trustworthy
- Good with money
- Detail oriented
- Has the time to devote to it
- Good communicator
- Organized
- Able to be neutral among beneficiaries and not favour one above another
- Motivated to get the job done
- Can get along with everyone in the family

It is alright for your executor to be a beneficiary of your estate as well. That is not a conflict of interest in law. Whether or not it would cause an issue in your particular family is another matter. The law cannot make your family get along with each other, so you will have to make some hard choices and realistic predictions about how your various family members would work together if you were to pass away.

For a related discussion, see chapter 6 regarding choosing a trustee to look after a testamentary trust for children.

There are various types of wills available, and they are designed to suit particular situations. As mentioned earlier, husbands and wives often get their wills made at the same time because they are jointly planning for the future protection of their children and assets. In such cases, they usually have "mirror" wills made. Mirror wills are so named because the wills of the husband and wife are the same as each other. The husband leaves everything to the wife, and vice versa, and their wills contain the same instructions for their estates when both of them have passed away.

For example, Andrew and Janet are married. Andrew's will says that he leaves everything to Janet, but if she has predeceased him, his estate is divided among their three children. Janet's will says that she leaves everything to Andrew, but if he has predeceased her, her estate is divided among their three children. Note that both Andrew and Janet are free to change their wills later if one of them is widowed, despite the popular misconception that they cannot.

Where does this leave you? If you and your spouse make mirror wills in which you leave all to each other, with matching plans for what will happen when both of you have died, your spouse is free to change his or her will after you die. In practice, it is the children of the couple who have made wills that have trouble with these mirror wills. For instance, looking at our example of Andrew and Janet above, if Andrew passed away, his estate would pass to Janet. If, a few years later, Janet remarried and then changed her will to include a new spouse, or to exclude one of her children, she is entitled to do so. However, the children may continue to talk about "Dad's estate" and "Dad's will" and "Dad's wishes" even though Andrew no longer has anything to do with it once the estate passes to Janet. It's a tough pill for the kids to swallow when Mom or Dad changes the will after one parent has died, but the law allows it.

This style of will is very frequently done, as the parents agree on the best plans for each other and their children. The mirror will is sometimes erroneously referred to a "mutual" will, though that is legally incorrect.

A mutual will may have elements in common with a mirror will, but the mutual will contains one thing that no other type of will contains; it has a clause in which both parties agree not to change their wills after the other one dies. It specifically says in the will document itself that neither of them will change their wills, and this becomes a valid contract between them. If a will does not have such a clause – and very few of them ever do - it is not a mutual will and the parties are free to change their wills after the other one has passed away.

Mutual wills are not done very often. The reason for that is simply that it is not very workable in real life for people never to change their wills after their spouse has died. For example, if Janet passed away and Andrew remarried, he would have a new legal obligation to his new spouse to include her in his estate. This would conflict directly with his will if it were prepared as a mutual will and he had agreed never to change it. There are some circumstances in which a mirror will would be suitable, but they are not the best choice for most people.

Another type of will that many people have heard of is the "joint" will. This is a single document that is the will for both a husband and a wife, almost as if they were one person. It was popular many years ago, but has long gone completely out of common usage. One of the main reasons for its demise is that it was based on the premise that all of the property in the marriage was owned by one person and therefore only one will was really needed. Though sometimes individuals ask whether their mirror wills are "joint" wills, they are not, because both husband and wife will have his or her own document.

Summary: There are several forms of wills available, all of which can be called "formal" wills. The term "formal" simply means that the document is not handwritten, and follows all of the formal will-signing requirements set out by law. In this section, the formal wills mentioned were:
- Mirror wills;
- Mutual wills; and
- Joint wills.

B. Hand-written will

The proper name for a hand-written will is "holograph" or "holographic" will. There are a couple of reasons that people want to make their own wills, mostly to do with the cost and inconvenience of seeing a lawyer to get a will made. Some people rationalize that because their affairs are simple, they don't need a lawyer. In other cases, illness or lack of mobility just makes it impossible for a person to get out to see a lawyer. Others live in small communities that may not have lawyers available.

A hand-written will has one major advantage over regular wills in terms of ease of preparation; in most jurisdictions it doesn't need witnesses. A person who makes a hand-written will can sign and date it, and it is valid without anyone needing to witness it.

The hand-written will is the type of will favoured by those who want to make their own wills, but it is unfortunately something that leads to an awful lot of mistakes. The worst part about making mistakes with your will is that you may never know you made a mistake, and it's only after you've died and your family tries to deal with your will that the error is discovered.

One of the major problems with hand-written wills is that they are not valid everywhere in Canada, and not everyone knows whether they live in an area that allows them. The table below lists each province and territory and shows whether that province or territory allows for hand-written wills to be legal. If you live in a province in which hand-written wills are not allowed, dying with a hand-written will is the same as dying with no will at all. In the last few years, more provinces and territories have updated their laws to allow for holographic wills and currently only British Columbia disallows them completely.

The next major problem with hand-written wills is that people are unclear as to exactly what qualifies as being hand-written. In order for a will to be holographic under the law, it must be 100% in the handwriting of the deceased, in addition to being properly signed and dated. In other places, such as Prince Edward Island and Nunavut, handwritten wills are allowed but they must have two witnesses. In other words, the rules are not simple and it's very easy to make a mistake that can invalidate your will.

Occasionally individuals will use a printed form, a packaged will kit, or a download from the internet into which they write certain names and information. Others will have a family member write out the will for them because their handwriting is tidier. These are not valid hand-written wills. This does not mean they cannot be valid wills. They can be valid if they are executed properly. The key to making a partially hand-written will valid is to treat it like a formal will and have it properly witnessed by two witnesses.

Table 3: *Jurisdictions that allow holographic wills*

Province or territory	*Are holograph wills valid?*
Alberta	Yes
British Columbia	No
Manitoba	Yes
New Brunswick	Yes
Newfoundland & Labrador	Yes
Northwest Territories	Yes
Nova Scotia	Yes
Nunavut	Yes, but two witnesses are still required
Ontario	Yes
Prince Edward Island	Yes, but two witnesses are still required
Quebec	Yes
Saskatchewan	Yes
Yukon	Yes

C. Codicil

A codicil is an amendment to an existing will. It is intended to make a small change when the will is otherwise suitable. For example, a codicil could be made if the will named an executor who moved to another country. The owner of the will might want to name a new person, but make no other changes to the will.

A codicil has all the same rules as a will when it comes to signing and witnessing. Once a codicil has been prepared and properly signed, it is attached to the will so that the two documents will be read together when the time comes.

Codicils became popular because before the advent of word processing and computers, new wills had to be typed out and before that, written out by hand. Codicils were quicker and easier to make than whole new wills. This meant that they were cheaper to prepare. For many years, consumers were able to save time and money by having codicils made instead of new wills.

However, times and technology change. Codicils have fallen out of favour and are rapidly becoming obsolete. This is happening for two main reasons.

The first reason is that people went too far with codicils. They would make as many or six or seven codicils to one will. This sometimes ended up creating absolute chaos. Some wills became incomprehensible because of codicils that contradicted or cancelled out each other and it will never be known whether those estates were actually carried out the way the deceased person really wanted. A codicil works perfectly well, but several codicils to a single will do not.

The second reason that codicils are less popular these days is that wills are now drafted on computers. When changes need to be made, it is no longer necessary to re-type the entire document because it has been saved on the computer. This means that it's actually cheaper and faster not to create a codicil, but simply to go into the existing will and change it.

A situation in which a codicil might be favoured over making a whole new will is that of an individual who wants to make a change but whose mental capacity may be declining. If the will was made years ago and there is no question about its validity, it might be a good idea to keep that will rather than prepare a new one. In that way, if lack of capacity is proven it will only affect the codicil and the person's original will is still safe.

D. Enduring Power of Attorney

An Enduring Power of Attorney is a document in which you choose someone to make decisions for you if one day you are no longer able to make those decisions for yourself. This document allows your chosen spokesperson (known as your "attorney") to make decisions regarding finances, property, lawsuits, and paperwork. It does not allow your attorney to make decisions regarding your health care.

The word "enduring" is vitally important. This means that the document has been made while the person giving it (known as the "donor") is mentally healthy and that the donor intends for the document to endure through any future mental incapacity. It shows that your document is indeed a planning tool that you set up in advance against the day when it might be needed.

Incapacity refers to the inability to make the decisions and carry out the transactions that most adults make on a regular basis. The incapacity can come about due to dementia, Alzheimer's disease, strong medications, injury, or illness. Most commonly, the Enduring Power of Attorney is prepared with aging and its possible loss of capacity in mind, but a serious accident or injury can happen to anyone at any age.

There are two basic types of Enduring Power of Attorney. The most common by far is the type that does not convey any power to anyone immediately, but comes into effect at some time in the future when the donor loses capacity. This type is sometimes referred to as a "springing" Enduring Power of Attorney because it springs into effect when it's needed. This type of document is so widespread because most of the individuals who sign these documents don't need any help with their finances or property at the time they sign the papers; they are simply planning ahead.

The springing type of document should state within it how it is to be brought into effect. The most common method of springing the document is for a doctor, or sometimes two doctors, to examine the donor and declare that he or she has lost the ability to deal with finances. There are options here. It's possible to have a family member involved in the assessment of incapacity if you wish. Some people find the involvement of a family member to be comforting. Others find it dangerous to give that kind of authority to a person who will one day inherit whatever is not spent during your lifetime. Each person has to make the decisions that seem best suited to themselves and their unique situation.

The other basic type of Enduring Power of Attorney is known as an "immediate" Enduring Power of Attorney. This type does not require an assessment of capacity to spring it into action because it is effective as soon as it is signed.

This type of document is less commonly done because of the issue of why a person who has the mental capacity to understand and sign an Enduring Power of Attorney would need help with finances. You might think that if the donor could do the former, he or she could quite well manage the latter, and to some extent that is correct.

An immediate Enduring Power of Attorney may be prepared by someone who is in the early stages of incapacity. Perhaps the person is functioning pretty well at the moment but is noticing some memory loss or confusion. If the doctor's prognosis is that the loss of capacity will continue and worsen, the donor might choose to get the Enduring Power of Attorney into place while he or she can still do so.

There may be good reasons other than the imminent onset of dementia for wanting to put an immediate Enduring Power of Attorney in place. For example, a person might feel perfectly fine mentally but have physical challenges that make such things as banking, shopping, and paperwork a real burden. He or she may wish to name an attorney now and work together with that named person.

The Enduring Power of Attorney is an extremely powerful document. When you sign this document, you are giving someone almost complete control over your finances, and therefore over how you live in the future. It allows the person you choose to do pretty much anything you could do with your money. Your attorney could sell your home or cabin, sell your car, re-invest your money, change banks, settle a lawsuit you're involved in, run or wind up your business, and deal with any contracts or agreements you've signed. It's a big job and you should be very careful to whom you give this power.

There are some things an attorney cannot legally do for you, such as:
- make a will for you;
- change your existing will;
- begin a divorce on your behalf;
- agree to a marriage on your behalf;
- cast your vote in an election.

However, your attorney will still have quite a bit of power over the way you live your life. Because of the amount of authority being conveyed by this document, you should be very careful in your choice of attorney. No matter who you choose, signing the document is a leap of faith, but you should try to be as practical and realistic as possible when evaluating your potential candidates.

Everyone who signs an Enduring Power of Attorney should take the steps they can to ensure that their attorney is doing the right things once they begin using the document. Your document should give some guidance on certain matters, and set out any specific items of concern to you. Remember that you likely won't have the mental capacity to give direction or explanations if someone is acting under your Power of Attorney, so make the document work for you. Here are some examples of specific matters addressed in Enduring Powers of Attorney:

- A direction not to sell the donor's cabin, boat, or vehicle because he or she intends to leave it to someone in his or her will;
- A direction to continue paying the tuition for a relative even though that relative is not a legal dependent;
- A direction to pay for the best long term care available for the donor;
- A direction to continue to give donations to the donor's church or favourite charity;
- A direction to continue to contribute to an RESP put into place for a grandchild;
- A direction that a particular family member who is not a legal dependent may continue to live in the donor's house rent-free.

The above list is not exhaustive by any means, but it should serve to illustrate the point that you can tailor your document to suit your own needs. To do this, think about what would happen in your family if you were taken out of commission by a traffic accident today. What are the things related to finances, paperwork, or property that you normally take care of that will not be done unless you appoint someone to do them?

Individuals who own businesses might consider having two Enduring Powers of Attorney at the same time. One would be strictly for business matters and the other strictly for personal matters. There would be a different attorney appointed under each document. This could work very well when the individual believes that his or her business partner is the best person to manage business matters such as hiring, firing, taking on contracts, payroll, paying bills, and attending directors' meetings. The individual would then make a separate Enduring Power of Attorney appointing his or her spouse or other family member to deal with private, personal matters such as the mortgage, the cabin, car loan, RRSP, and personal bank accounts.

In some cases, a person's spouse or children are also involved in the business and would be perfectly fine handling both the business and personal finances, but not in all cases. For a business owner who wants to keep the two worlds separate, having two Enduring Powers of Attorney may be appropriate. If this arrangement is used, the drafting of the documents must be done carefully to ensure that the two can peacefully and effectively co-exist.

Your attorney is bound by law always to act in your best interests, even when his or her interests are in direct conflict with yours. However, this is a pretty tough standard and not everyone can meet it. Some don't even try. Unfortunately, fraud, embezzlement, and even downright negligence often lead to financial loss for the donor due to the actions of his or her appointed attorney. These days, the trend is towards including clauses in the document that are intended to protect the donor. Ironically, it is the very people who need protection that are the most reluctant to accept this type of clause in their documents, that is, the overly-trusting parents.

Many parents strongly resist including anything at all in their Enduring Power of Attorney that might even hint that they don't trust the person they've put in charge, or that the named person is not perfect. Somehow it is more important to them to avoid offending that person than it is to avoid losing all of their assets. Though that may sound harsh, it is true that the majority of elder financial abuse happens at the hands of trusted family members. Parents assume that they will be safe in the hands of their children, as do aunts, uncles, and grandparents, but sadly they are often proved wrong. Because of their reluctance to protect themselves from their children, they are even more vulnerable than they would be to strangers.

One of the few protective clauses that parents will gladly accept is the requirement that the person named as attorney must give regular financial reports to others in the family. Usually this happens when a parent has a number of children but only one is named as the attorney. If this clause is included, once the child begins working under the Enduring Power of Attorney document, he or she is required to give a full, written report of all activities and current values on an annual basis to his or her siblings.

This is acceptable to parents not so much because of the transparency needed to help combat fraud, but because they feel they are keeping the rest of the kids in the loop and not leaving them out. It doesn't feel as if it casts a negative light on the chosen child, so it seems more acceptable.

One of the ways in which this clause is extremely useful is to keep the siblings apprised of how the parent's estate diminishes over time, particularly if the parent is in a care facility. The children tend to think that "Mom had money" and are appalled and suspicious when the parent passes away and there is a lot less in the estate than they had expected. This almost always causes them to turn viciously on the child who had been acting under the Power of Attorney. They forget the high cost of care has eaten into the parent's money. However, when an annual report is provided, there is less likelihood of any surprises. The siblings can see each year how the cost of care and other expenses reduce the estate. If they have an issue, they can raise it early on, rather than finding out years later when it may be too late to do anything about it.

Another helpful clause that may gain traction in the future is a requirement that any child who is named as the attorney may only begin acting under the Enduring Power of Attorney once he or she has consulted a lawyer to learn about the authorities and limits of the role. The fact that they had complied with the requirement would be evidenced by a letter or certificate provided by the lawyer to show that the attorney had attended a meeting for that purpose. The cost of the meeting would be covered by the donor (parent) so that it did not present a barrier to anyone named as attorney.

This clause would be very helpful simply because it would help prevent the kind of serious errors that many attorneys make. Let's face it, not all losses to the parents happen because a child is deliberately greedy or fraudulent. Sometimes it happens by accident because the child had no real idea of what to do. There is no formal training out there for adult kids who suddenly become the attorney for their parents, so they are learning on the job. Plenty of them make expensive mistakes despite their best intentions, to the detriment of their parents' finances. Having a meeting with a lawyer who can discuss what to do and what to avoid would be quite valuable. Not many lawyers are yet suggesting this kind of clause for Enduring Powers of Attorney, other than lawyers who specialize in this area of law, but the use of these clauses will become more widespread.

The decision around who to appoint under your Enduring Power of Attorney should be made carefully. When considering who to name as attorney, keep in mind that it's a difficult job, time-consuming, and one that is, frankly, thankless most of the time. It also allows someone direct access to everything you own, so it carries an enormous amount of responsibility.

A good choice for your attorney is someone who is:
- Geographically accessible;
- Good with money;
- Sensible, level-headed, and patient;
- Honest and trustworthy;
- Detail-oriented;
- Able to devote the time needed;
- Able to get along with all the members of your family;
- Willing to work with you to the extent that you're able;
- Not in a situation in which access to money would be a temptation.

Most individuals, logically enough, choose family members as their attorneys. Spouses generally choose each other. One or more of the kids are the usual second choice. However, it's not essential that your representative be a family member if you don't have anyone who has the necessary skills and time and who also happens to live nearby. While it is perfectly legal to appoint someone who lives outside of your province, doing so will add to the costs being charged to you once the person begins acting on your behalf.

An option for some people is a trust company. Because the job of attorney is a financial one, a trust company can be a good fit if there are significant assets to be looked after. Though many families look only at the cost of a trust company and immediately dismiss the idea of using one, the better idea is to look at the value. The real value of using a trust company is the neutrality that will avoid mistakes, avoid favoritism, avoid embezzlement, and ultimately save you money and save your family from disputes.

Trust companies charge an annual fee for their services in the range of 1 to 2% of the assets they are managing. If you are curious about what a trust company could do for you and what it would charge, you can call up any trust company and ask for information. Making the call doesn't obligate you to hire them. The major banks in Canada have trust companies attached to them, so your first enquiry should probably be in the branch where you do your usual banking.

E. Healthcare Directive

A healthcare directive goes by many names, depending on where you live. It is also called a Personal Directive, Power of Attorney for Personal Care, or Advance Directive. In this book, the generic term "healthcare directive" is used, but it refers to any and all of these documents.

A healthcare directive is a document in which an individual names a person of his or her choice as a health care agent. If the individual should at any future time lose his or her ability to make medical or personal decisions, the agent may step in and make those decisions. The healthcare directive should contain some instructions for the agent to assist the agent in making decisions that support the individual's values and wishes. For example, the healthcare directive should describe the individual's instructions to his or her agent on what to do if the individual is in a vegetative state and is being kept alive only by artificial means.

The healthcare directive should be tailored to the individual's wishes. There should be a frank, open discussion about what the individual wants for his or her future care so that anyone who acts under the document has some help making decisions. Some examples of specific instructions that could be included in a healthcare directive are:
- If the individual is averse to going to a long-term care facility in the future, an instruction to the agent to keep him or her at home, with appropriate help and support, as long as possible;
- An instruction that if the individual is going to live in a long-term care facility, that it be a place that

allows him or her to carry on his or her faith (for example, kosher food or proximity to a place of worship);
- Allowing organ donation after death;
- Restrictions on the type of treatment that is acceptable, such as the refusal of blood transfusions.

When personalizing a healthcare directive, it is important to get the wording just right to ensure that your instructions are clearly understood. One particular item that causes a great deal of confusion is the use of the Do Not Resuscitate (DNR) instruction. Most people think this means something that it simply does not mean.

DNR is an instruction to medical staff not to revive you under any circumstances. Most people who say they want their documents to say DNR are thinking about a situation in which they are dying of an incurable disease, or are being kept alive artificially by a machine. However, the part that people miss is that the DNR instruction is not just for that. It's for all situations. For instance, you could have a stroke or mild heart attack. Given proper medical care, you could be expected to recover and live for many more productive years. However, with a DNR on your directive, you are refusing that care and may end up shortening your life by many years for no good reason.

When this is explained to people, they usually hasten to say that they didn't mean for the DNR to apply to those situations. They just want it to be used in dire circumstances. However, he medical staff are not going to stand around debating whether your particular situation is one in which you "really" mean for your directive to apply.

It's up to you to understand what your instructions mean and to state them so that other people can follow them. Don't use "DNR" as a blanket instruction unless you really do mean to refuse any and all medical care under all circumstances.

If that isn't what you want, talk to a lawyer about drafting a healthcare directive that will ensure that your end-of-life wishes not to be kept alive artificially are not accidentally applied in other circumstances.

The benefit to any individual of having a healthcare directive is that the individual can retain some control over what happens even if he or she cannot speak. The choice of agent alone is a huge benefit, as the individual can choose someone that he or she trusts, as opposed to the courts choosing someone they believe is appropriate. Once you appoint someone, you can hold a conversation with him or her to talk about your wishes and beliefs.

Recent developments in Canadian law have allowed those who are in extreme pain due to illness and whose condition is both incurable and intolerable to request that a physician assist him or her to end their life. This has led a number of people to ask whether such a decision could be included in a healthcare directive so that the request for end of life assistance is made in advance.

This is not possible at present. Each of the provinces has set up guidelines (some of which are still subject to adjustment) that address the question of who can request physician-assisted death and under what circumstances the request can be made. The various jurisdictions are unanimous on the fact that the decision cannot be made in advance, nor can it be made by someone else on behalf of the person who is suffering. The person making the request has to have mental capacity to understand the request in the circumstances as they are happening. The healthcare directive, on the other hand, is only used when a person does *not* have capacity to make decisions. Therefore the healthcare directive cannot request physician-assisted dying.

A person who acts for you under your healthcare directive cannot be paid for those services.

F. Memorandum to executor

A Memorandum to your executor is a letter that you leave with your will, addressed to your executor or trustee, which is not going to be read until you pass away. In it, you may leave further instructions, or an explanation of why you set things up the way you did. You can talk about anything you like, though you do have to be careful that you don't contradict anything in your will, or add new gifts that aren't in your will. It's a place for expressing emotions, leaving personal messages, or simply giving more information about your estate plan.
Some of the ideas often expressed in memoranda to executors are:
- An explanation as to why a certain inheritance was held in trust;
- An explanation as to why a certain person was left out of the will;
- A wish that the children be brought up in a particular faith;
- A wish that the children be mentored and taught by the executor about money so that they will one

day be able to handle their inheritance properly;
- An explanation about why the executor was chosen to be executor;
- Funeral or burial wishes;
- Guidelines about how the executor is going to handle the estate trusts for children (e.g. generously vs. strictly);
- Confirmation of whether property jointly owned with a child is intended to go to the child by right of survivorship, or whether the child was simply added to the title for convenience or economy;
- Suggestions of people who can be called upon by the executor for advice or support;
- Personal messages of love, regret, or support.

G. Memorandum of Personal Effects

In your will, you may choose to leave specific items to certain people. The items may be of financial or sentimental value, as you see fit. Many individuals like to leave special pieces of jewelry such as a wedding band, or special family heirlooms such as photographs or antiques. This is partly to ensure that the importance of those items is not overlooked, and partly to ensure that there are no disputes over who should receive them.

Including such items in a will is a good idea, but it has one drawback. If you change your mind about giving the item or if you dispose of the item during your lifetime, your will is no longer accurate. To keep your will accurate and current, you would have to make changes to it whenever you changed your mind about the individual items. This is inconvenient and could get expensive.

There is an alternative method of disposing of household and personal items that may be easier for many people. This alternate method is known as a "Memorandum of Personal Effects". It is essentially a list of names with a list of items each person would receive. It is a separate document from your will but is intended to be used along with your will to give additional information and direction to your executor.

The benefit of using a Memorandum of Personal Effects is that it is flexible. It can be prepared before you make your will or afterwards. You can change your mind at any time and add to the list or subtract from it. You must sign and date it, but it does not require witnesses. Because of its flexibility and ease of use, the Memorandum has always been a popular tool for those doing their estate planning.

There are some drawbacks to using the Memorandum of Personal Effects, most of which are a result of human error in preparing the document. The main error made by those using the document is a lack of clarity about who and what are described in the Memorandum. For example, a man might leave something to "Joe" in his Memorandum. He knows who he means, but it may not be clear to others reading it after his passing if he has a brother named Joseph, a nephew called Joe Junior, and a grandson called Joey. It is easy to forget that when the document is used, you won't be around to clarify any muddy parts. You have to write the Memorandum in such a way that it can be read and understood by others.

The other place in which clarity is often missing is in the description of items. If a woman makes a Memorandum in which she leaves her ring to her daughter, but she owns several rings, it may not be clear which ring she meant to give. The descriptions used are often of little help, since they may say things like "my favourite ring" or "the ring I bought when I was on vacation". Again, those are descriptions that are only clear to the person writing them, and not to the executor or the family member who are dealing with the estate. They should have been written in a way that others could use.

Lack of clarity leads to disputes, mistakes, and hurt feelings.

A Memorandum of Personal Effects may only be used to give personal and household goods. That is a pretty wide description, and includes anything that is normally found in your home, cabin, garden, sheds, or vehicle. Even vehicles and boats may be included, as well as accessories such as trailers. The most commonly named items are jewelry, family heirlooms, artwork, tools, and special items such as antiques. It can be used to divide up a house full of furniture, or to make sure that each person gets a memento. It can suit a variety of needs.

There are limits to what may be given in a Memorandum of Personal Effects. You cannot leave sums of money or bank accounts. You cannot leave real estate of any kind. If money or real estate are left in the Memorandum, it may amount in law to a new will and may revoke the will you have in place. Alternatively, the court may disallow the Memorandum.

In order to avoid disputes and delays, list only household and personal items, and be as clear as you can about who you are benefitting and what you want to give to them.

Some people like to include photographs of the items in their list, and that is acceptable.

Because this document is intended to be a sort of supplement to your will, it should be mentioned in your will. There are two ways to do that, and they have very different outcomes.

The first way to mention a Memorandum of Personal Effects in a will is to "incorporate it by reference". This means that in the will, there will be a paragraph that refers to the Memorandum and identifies it as being a certain document that was signed on a certain day. When a Memorandum is incorporated by reference into the will, it becomes as cast in stone as the rest of your will. It becomes a part of the will and your executor must follow it just as he must follow any other part of the will. However, it has the same drawback as including the items in the will in the first place, which is that you have lost the flexibility to make changes without changing your will.

The second way to mention a Memorandum of Personal Effects in a will is simply that – to mention it and say that you may make a Memorandum. This alerts your executor to look for a Memorandum. While this retains the desired flexibility in terms of the ability to change your wishes, it also means that the Memorandum has not been given the full force of the law as it would had it been incorporated by reference. A Memorandum that has not been incorporated by reference is only upheld and followed if all of the residuary beneficiaries of the estate agree to that.

When deciding whether a Memorandum of Personal Effects is suitable for you and whether or not it should be incorporated by reference, talk it over with your estate lawyer.

H. Shareholders' Agreement

Though a shareholders' agreement is by nature and definition a corporate document, it is also an important estate planning tool for business owners. A shareholders' agreement will cover many different topics and scenarios, but for the purpose of this discussion, there are two main issues that a shareholders' agreement should touch on. Those are the death of the shareholder and the future incapacity of the shareholder. The agreement should be specific about what will happen with the shares owned by the shareholder if he or she passes away or becomes incompetent.

When an individual dies, his or her assets are distributed according to his or her will. If the individual's assets include shares in a privately owned company, those shares will be given to the beneficiaries just like any other asset. Typically, a shareholders' agreement will provide that these shares will be bought back by the company. This is done so that the shareholders can maintain control over the ownership of the company.

The terms of the agreement would provide that the company would offer the beneficiary who inherited the shares fair market value for the shares. To ensure that the company has the money on hand to make this buy-back, the company will most likely own an insurance policy on the life of each shareholder. When the shareholder dies, the insurance company pays the benefit to the company. The company then uses the insurance money to buy the deceased's shares from the estate or the beneficiary.

This is pretty standard procedure for small and medium sized businesses, but it does require the shareholders to take the time to put the agreement together and place the insurance policies.

The procedure to be followed when a shareholder loses mental capacity is in theory very similar but in practice is much more difficult. There are two stumbling blocks. The first is the actual determination of incapacity. Incapacity is not always obvious and it may be something that happens gradually. Therefore it may be tricky to know when, officially, it's time to invoke the buy-back terms of the agreement.

One possible solution to that particular issue is to state that the buy-back terms would come into effect if the shareholder's Enduring Power of Attorney has been called into effect. The drawback is that, of course, it is dependent upon the shareholder preparing an Enduring Power of Attorney in advance, and on the person named to step up and assume responsibility, and on the willingness of a physician to make a declaration of incapacity.

The second stumbling block is the availability of funds to purchase the shares. Unlike in the case of the death of the shareholder, the onset of incapacity does not trigger the payment of life insurance. Therefore the company would have to rely on some other source of funds to purchase the shares. The purchase would not be made from the shareholder's estate, but from the shareholder himself by way of the person acting under his or her Enduring Power of Attorney.

The bottom line for business owners is that when the company has more than one shareholder, it takes some planning and cooperation between the shareholders to ensure that they protect the company and their estates.

CHAPTER 5: UNDERSTANDING YOUR PERSONAL ESTATE PLAN PUZZLE

Many people believe that "estate planning" really means getting a will made. To some extent, that's true, as a will is the backbone of your estate plan. However, planning your estate has much more to it than just making a will. The most useful way to think of estate planning is to imagine it's a puzzle, and you want to put all the pieces together. The will might be the biggest piece, but it's not the only piece. As you have seen in the previous chapter of this book, there are other documents that should be prepared along with your will, because they do different jobs than your will does. They complement and strengthen each other.

The difference between planning your estate and having a will done is really the difference between not leaving problems for your family to sort out after you're gone and simply letting the problems build up. By ensuring that all of the pieces of your particular puzzle fit together, you can avoid confusion and resentment by your beneficiaries, and prevent lawsuits and family fights.

If you do not consider all aspects of your estate puzzle together, you run a sizeable risk that you will end up leaving instructions that contradict each other, or leaving gaps in your plans. One item might make perfect sense on its own, but cause confusion when placed next to other estate documents. In this chapter, you are encouraged to view your estate as one large item made up of various interlocking parts.

Here is a common example of an incomplete estate plan that many readers will find familiar. Anna is a widowed woman who makes a will that says that all of her three children are to receive equal shares of her estate when she passes away. Then she adds one of her children to her bank account, making the child a joint owner. Anna doesn't think that the bank account has anything to do with her will or the instructions for her estate. When Anna dies, the child on the bank account claims it as under a joint owner's right of survivorship and does not share it because joint assets do not fall into an estate. The other two children are outraged, since Anna's will says everyone is to get the same amount. The dispute ends up in court, costing the estate money, and ruining the relationship between the children forever.

The above example happens a dozen times every day in every province and territory in Canada. If Anna had planned her estate thoroughly instead of just making a will, her children would not now be fighting among themselves and taking her estate to court. She should have talked to the estate planning lawyer about the joint bank account. Anna should have explained the goal she was trying to achieve, and let the lawyer help her put those pieces together in a workable way.

Below, you will find a list of several assets and arrangements that are owned or held by many Canadians. You will probably have a few of them yourself. The purpose of this chapter is to give you some information about these items so that you will become aware that your estate plan is much more than simply your will. Everything you set up at the bank or with your financial advisor must work with your will as none of these things exist in isolation. By reading the information here, you will see how each asset or arrangement works so you can understand how they impact each other and your will. Hopefully you will see that if these various items are not all taken together, some can accidentally contradict the others or create doubt about your intentions.

A. Designated beneficiaries

Some financial assets can be left directly to a certain person without the funds going through your estate. When you leave such an asset to a beneficiary by naming the person at the time you buy or set up the asset, it is called "designating" a beneficiary. Some examples are:
- Life insurance
- Registered Retirement Savings Plans (RRSPs)
- Registered Retirement Income Funds (RRIFs)
- Pensions

These items don't become part of your estate when you pass away because you have already named ("designated") someone to receive the funds. This is a contract that you have with the bank or insurance company that acts independently of your will. When you pass away, the funds go directly to the named person and are not handled by your executor. They are not controlled by your will.

If the person you have designated has died before you, the funds fall into your estate. If that happens, then they are covered by your will. When looking at your estate planning puzzle, remember that the proceeds of your plans, pensions, and policies are not covered by your will if you name a beneficiary and that beneficiary outlives you.

If you make a will that leaves your estate equally to your children, for example, consider how that equal division is impacted if you leave assets to one of the children by way of a beneficiary designation. It may cause confusion among the children if they are expecting everyone to receive the same thing and one child receives an additional amount from a designated asset.

For example, Fred makes a will leaving his two daughters his estate in equal shares. He had a life insurance policy that named his wife, but after his wife died, he changed it to name his older daughter. When Fred dies, his will is going to split everything he owns equally, except for the life insurance policy. That will be paid by the insurance company right to his daughter. This means that the two daughters are getting the same amount under the will, but one is still getting more than the other because she also has the life insurance money. Is this what Fred intended? His will suggest that it's not, but his beneficiary designation suggests that it is.

Many people make the mistake of assuming that the executor they name will "figure it out" or fix the problem, but that is not the case. Executors don't have the legal authority to change the distribution under the will because they think it might be poorly written; they must do what the will says and nothing more or less. An executor cannot change the designation you make on an insurance policy or financial plan.

If Fred wanted his daughters to share the life insurance policy, he should have changed the beneficiary to name his estate so that it would have been divided under the will. If, on the other hand, he wanted his oldest daughter to own the policy proceeds for herself, he could have used his will to confirm the beneficiary designation with a brief statement of his intentions. Either of those steps would have cleared up the confusion.

It is possible to use your will to change a beneficiary designation but that is not always an effective way to make the desired change. This is because the insurance company or bank that holds your plan or account will not know about the provisions of your will or the change you've made, and will most likely pay out the proceeds of the plan or account to the beneficiary they know about. Then your executor will be in a position of having to try to get the funds back from the person they were paid to, which generally involves a lawsuit. A better way to make a change is to go directly to the bank or insurance company and make the change on the original account or policy.

B. Registered Education Savings Plans

Registered Education Savings Plans, or RESPs, are given their own section in this chapter simply because they do not behave at all the way RRSPs or RRIFs do. Though the majority of people assume that on death, the money in RESPs goes to the beneficiaries named, it does not.

If you own an RESP for your child or grandchild and you are the only owner of that plan, on your death the RESP is collapsed and money goes into your regular estate along with the rest of your assets. It will then be divided according to your will. An RESP usually has some funds that came from the government, and on your death those funds must be repaid to the government, along with any income made on the funds.

No doubt this is not how you pictured the RESP working. An awful lot of people are taken by surprise by this information, and so are their family members who were counting on the funds to pay for someone's education. The good news is that it is very easy to prevent this situation by putting the right clause in your will.

The way to prevent the collapse of the RESP and to ensure that the plan continues on for the benefit of your child or grandchild is to ensure that there is someone who will own the plan if you are no longer around to own it. If you are the only owner of the plan, either add another owner to it while you are alive, or put a clause in your will to name someone who will own the plan when you're gone (known as a "successor owner").

You can name your spouse as the successor owner, or you can name the executor and trustee of your estate as the successor owner, or any other person that you trust.

The successor owner does not become the named beneficiary. That will stay the same; if you've named your child or grandchild as the beneficiary, they will still be named. The successor owner is someone who will be the custodian of the money just as you are during your lifetime.

C. Life insurance

Although life insurance was mentioned in the previous section of this chapter because it is an item that designates a beneficiary, it warrants a section of its own to discuss how and why it can be used in estate planning.

When you go through the estate planning process, you should end up with a good idea of what sort of tax bill your estate will incur. You will at least know which assets are taxable (for example, your cabin or rental property) and how to estimate what the taxes on them will be. For help estimating your tax exposure, see Chapter 7 of this book.

Once you know what your taxes will likely be, and you have taken reasonable steps to limit those taxes, such as using rollovers where available, you should look at your overall estate to see what assets you will have available to pay the portion of the taxes that cannot be avoided. For some people, the answer to paying their estate taxes is life insurance.

Having life insurance that is payable to your estate when you pass away is a method of creating new cash in your estate that can be used for paying debts and expenses, including tax. Not everyone needs to create new cash. If your estate already contains liquid assets, those may well be enough to pay your expenses and taxes without any assets having to be sold.

If, on the other hand, your estate contains several pieces of real estate and almost no liquid assets, you must realize that without extra cash, some or all of the properties may have to be sold to pay the taxes. If you were planning for those properties to be sold anyway, this is likely not a concern, but if you were hoping to leave those properties to individuals in your will, you may need the extra cash to avoid sale of the properties. Remember that beneficiaries cannot legally be paid their inheritance until all bills and taxes are paid, so not having enough cash in the estate can really upset your estate plan.

The cost of buying a new life insurance policy may be prohibitive for some people, but it's an idea worth considering for those whose estates contain very few liquid assets.

The extra cash created by a life insurance policy can be used for more than paying taxes. It can be extremely useful when a parent wants to treat all of his or her children equally but the bulk of the estate is tied up in one asset. For example, the parent may have two children and an estate with an overall value of $1,000,000. Though the parent wants to treat the children equally, this is difficult because the family business, which he wants to leave to his daughter, is worth $750,000 and there are not enough other assets to give his son the same amount of inheritance as the daughter. In a case like this, the funds from an insurance policy could be used to create cash to pay to the son who is not getting the family business.

The same principle applies if one child is receiving rental properties or the family home or other major asset and the parent wants to try to equalize the inheritance of the other children.

D. Joint property

There is a general rule in law that when two or more people own an asset as joint owners, there is a right of survivorship (with some exceptions, as discussed in the next section of this chapter). This means that when one owner dies, the other owner automatically gets to own the entire property. Joint ownership is a last man standing arrangement because whoever outlives the other owner(s) eventually gets to own the asset outright. For most people, the assets that are put into joint names are real estate and bank accounts.

It's important to understand that you can have more than one name on an asset without that asset being jointly owned. Assuming that there is joint ownership just because more than one name appears on the title is a mistake that has caught out many testators, causing them to make invalid gifts in their wills and leaving their beneficiaries in confusion.

An asset can be held as "tenants-in-common". This involves having two or more owners on the title, but there is no right of survivorship. With tenants-in-common, each person owns half of the asset (or a third, or whatever arrangement was agreed upon at the time the asset was purchased). When that owner passes away, his or her share of the asset is dealt with under their will.

As an example, let's look at Lisa and Josie, two sisters who want to buy a house together as a rental property to earn income. They are going to put down approximately the same amount of deposit, and they will share the mortgage payments more or less equally as well. They are debating whether they should be joint owners or tenants-in-common.

If they decide to be joint owners and one of them should die, the other will own the entire property. If Lisa, the older sister, passes away first, no part of the house will be in her estate, so there is nothing that would pass to her husband and children. Anything she had put into the property, such as her share of the down payment, will be gone.

On the other hand, if the sisters had decided to own the house as tenants-in-common and Lisa passed away, her half of the house becomes part of her estate. She can control through her will who gets her half. Realistically, either Josie would buy her out (because it's pretty tough to sell half a house on the open market) or the entire property would be sold so that the money could be split between them.

The tenants-in-common arrangement would work for the people in this example. It's not nearly as common as the joint property arrangement simply because most couples, either married or common law, arrange to have joint property in order to ensure that the survivor of them will be sure to keep their home.

During the estate planning process, if you are unsure about whether you are a joint owner or a tenant-in-common, it is a very good idea to check on this before deciding your plans. This can be done simply and quickly, even if you do not know where the deed to your home might be. You can go to the local land titles registry and do a search of the title for only a few dollars. If you find the title itself confusing or unclear, take it to your wills lawyer and ask for clarification of exactly where you stand with the title.

There is an extremely important exception to the rule that a joint owner of an asset will inherit the asset by right of survivorship. That exception exists where a parent adds the name of one of his or her children, grandchildren, nieces, or nephews to an asset. This exception will be discussed in detail in the next section of this chapter.

E. Intergenerational joint property

As mentioned in the previous section of this chapter, there is an exception to the rule that a surviving joint tenant automatically gains ownership of an asset. The exception exists in the following circumstances:
- The asset – whether bank account, investment portfolio or real estate – was originally owned by a parent or grandparent;
- The parent or grandparent added the name of a child, grandchild, niece, or nephew to the property or account as a joint owner;
- The person who was added did not contribute money to the asset;
- The reason for adding the new person is to avoid probate, to keep probate fees low, for convenience, or to ensure the kids have money to pay expenses when the parent or grandparent passes away.

If this sounds familiar, it's because hundreds of thousands of Canadians have done this and continue to do this. Parents and grandparents add someone from the next generation to the title of their home or to their bank accounts all the time. Sadly, it is a bigger mistake than most of them will ever know. Only the kids or grandchildren who have to sort it out later will realize what a terrible idea it was. The fact that the law has changed just isn't widely known and thousands of Canadians don't realize the impact of their actions.

In a situation as described above, the child or grandchild who has been added to the asset is no longer automatically entitled to the asset because of the right of survivorship. As of 2007, the law states that an asset that fits the above description must be held in trust for the estate of the parent or grandparent until evidence is found of the parent's or grandparent's intention for the inheritance of the property.

At this point, many people suggest that the fact that it has been put into joint names is evidence that the parent wants the child to inherit as a joint owner. However, the law is clear that the mere fact of putting into joint names is not enough evidence. As we have just discussed, there are many reasons why parents and grandparents add their children and grandchildren to their assets and most of those reasons are NOT so that the child or grandchild can inherit. The legal concept of joint ownership was not intended to allow for probate avoidance and similar arrangements, so the change to the law helps clarify that using it to achieve those ends is pushing a square peg into a round hole. No wonder it doesn't fit properly.

Another factor to take into consideration is the fact that not all families are lovely, gentle, compassionate groups of people. Some children and grandchildren are more than willing to force, persuade, frighten, or trick their elders into adding their names to assets in the hopes of financial gain. Though it is disturbing to think about, the majority of elder financial abuse in our country is perpetuated by the close family members of the abused individuals, and one of the favourite ways of taking assets away from parents and grandparents is to be added as a joint owner.

In other words, our legal system has decided to make it a little more difficult for some of those perpetrators to get away with it.

Now when a parent or grandparent passes away with a joint asset that fits the test set out above, the question that must be asked is: Why did this person add someone as a joint owner? There are only two possible answers to the question:
a – because he or she wanted the joint owner to inherit the asset for himself/herself to keep; or
b – any other reason.

If the answer is "a", that the surviving joint owner would keep the asset for himself or herself, then it's a "true" joint ownership and the surviving joint owner gets to keep the asset.

If the answer is "b", then the asset in question is part of the deceased's estate and is covered by the will. The surviving joint owner does NOT get to keep it.

As you can see, this means that most of the people who have added someone to an asset – usually the family home – to try to keep it out of probate or to lower the fees are going to fail in reaching that goal. The law says that the property is still in the estate. Anyone who adds a child to a bank account for convenience or to ensure there is money for the funeral, or because that child "knows who I want them to give it to" is also going to fall short of the goal. Those accounts are still in the account.

This is not at all the way people think this works, which is why there is so much confusion and contradiction and arguing when someone passes away after adding a joint owner to an asset. To add to the confusion, some banks are not up to date on the law and are wrongly paying out joint bank accounts to surviving inter-generational joint owners. In my opinion, this will continue to happen until a disappointed beneficiary realizes a bank's misuse of the funds and sues for the amount he or she did not inherit.

This brings the discussion back around to the issue of evidence. In order to determine what the parent or grandparent intended for the joint asset, there has to be some independent evidence left by the parent. As you can imagine, this is rarely done for the simple reason that nobody knows they are supposed to leave such evidence.

There are very few ways for a parent or grandparent to leave such evidence. Verbal instructions to someone to divide up an account or to keep the house or any other such instructions are not valid. The evidence required must be in writing, must have been left by the parent of grandparent who added someone to the asset, and in most cases must have been made around the same time as the person was added to the title.

One very easy way that is surprisingly under-used is simply to confirm your intentions in your will. A one-line sentence in your will could read either "I confirm that I have added my daughter, Jean, to the title of my home because I want Joan to own the home for herself", or the opposite, "I confirm that my daughter Joan has been added to my investment portfolio in order to help me to manage the account while I am alive, but that account is intended to form part of my estate." One of the main reasons this book treats your estate documents and assets as a puzzle that must fit together is that your various items should support and improve each other. Using your will to clarify a joint ownership arrangement is simple and effective.

There are not many other places to look for such supporting evidence. One such place is the bank at which the parent or grandparent held the account to which someone was added. If you are very lucky, the bank personnel who set up the account might have asked why the child or grandchild was being added, and might have recorded the answer. It's a long shot, but it has paid off for some estates. If the banking officer had recorded a note saying, for example, "Mrs. Jones is no longer very mobile and needs help with banking so she is adding her son", then there is no longer any need to guess what Mrs. Jones intended with that account.

Another possibility is to find out what was recorded by the lawyer who drew the will. Perhaps the deceased talked to the lawyer about what he or she wanted to do with the asset in question. This is not easy to access by any means because a lawyer's duty of confidentiality to his or her client carries on even when the client has passed away. However, if there is a trial in court about the deceased's asset in question, the lawyer's notes may be accessed by way of subpoena.

Keep in mind that while the search for evidence is under way and the discussions are going on, the estate simply sits in limbo. Nobody gets their share of the estate until it is clear what is actually in the estate. And of course, while this is going on, the children are taking sides and arguing about who is going to keep the asset. If matters cannot be resolved between the executor and the beneficiaries amicably – and often they cannot – then it may take the intervention of the courts to make a determination on what to do with the assets.

Anyone who thinks adding a child or grandchild to their home to save on probate fees should think about the cost of the lawsuit it may take to straighten out the estate later on.

The caution against adding a child or grandchild to an asset is something that many individuals choose to ignore. They feel that because it is happening among all of their friends and family, it must be okay. Unfortunately, all they hear is someone saying they've added their kids to their house to avoid probate. It seems like a reasonable idea to them. What they don't hear is the kids' side of the story, years later, when the parent passes away. Estate planning lawyers continue to spread the word that adding a child to an asset is NOT a way to avoid probate, but the practice is well-entrenched and it's going to take a long time for public awareness to catch up to reality.

F. Divorce or separation

Divorce or separation arrangements may require you to carry out certain steps that impact your overall estate planning. For example, you may be required to carry a life insurance policy that names your former spouse as the beneficiary. If that is the case, your obligation will outlive you. If you change the beneficiary of the life insurance policy so that on your death your former spouse does not receive the proceeds of the policy you were ordered to make or agreed to make, he or she will likely challenge your estate to get funds equal to the policy proceeds. Your estate will most likely end up paying your former spouse the proceeds of the policy, and legal costs as well as the law would be on the side of your former spouse.

There is an aspect of divorce and/or separation that often causes problems with estates, and this error can be fixed by you during the estate planning process. Much like the pre-nuptial agreements discussed elsewhere in this book, a typical agreement between separating parties contains a statement to the effect that neither of them will make a claim against the estate of the other. It also says that all property that's going to be divided has been divided so that everyone is content with the division and won't claim anything else. This often leads individuals to conclude that the former spouse simply cannot and will not get anything from the estate. They are wrong.

Signing an agreement like that does not change beneficiary designations. Nor does it change joint property titles. Those are separate steps that you must take yourself as part of your property division. For example, while you are married you may have a life insurance policy that names your spouse as your beneficiary. When you separate or divorce, you divide up your assets and eventually you both sign an agreement that you have dealt with all matrimonial property. Your paperwork includes the clause that neither will claim on each other's estate. However, you forget to change the beneficiary on the policy. When you pass away, the policy will still be paid to your former spouse. The signing of the separation agreement does not prevent that, nor does an order of divorce from the court. Receiving the life insurance from you is not a claim on your estate by your ex, as the life insurance was never in your estate.

Unfortunately, many people forget to change beneficiary designations for the simple reason that during the property division process they have so many details to remember that occasionally one slips past them. This is another reason why making a new will after a divorce or separation is a good idea, as the forgotten policy will most likely be noticed during the will planning process, giving you a chance to bring it up to date.

It should also be noted that in general, getting a divorce does not revoke your will, nor does signing a separation agreement. The will you made while married will continue to be in effect until you replace it or revoke it. This could mean that your carefully negotiated property division is completely negated if your estate is left to the person you just divorced. In some parts of Canada, your divorce does not invalidate your will, but the parts of your will that give your estate to your former spouse are revoked. This is a realistic response to the issue, to some extent, but it is not yet the law everywhere. Check Table 4 in chapter 8 for a summary of how the laws of the difference provinces deal with wills on divorce.

G. Prenuptial agreement

If you have signed a prenuptial agreement or co-habitation agreement, it is most likely going to impact your estate planning. In fact, that is one of the main purposes of such an agreement. Though the prenuptial agreement does not replace a will, it does contain provisions that decide where some of your property will go on your death.

In general, a prenuptial agreement will state that on the death of one of the parties, each will keep what he or she brought into the relationship and that they will split the property that they acquired together. Most agreements get quite specific, naming individual pieces of furniture or jewelry that one party may keep.

In the context of estate planning, you cannot give away in your will any items that you have already agreed will belong to your spouse on your death. The prenuptial agreement is a valid contract and is intended to survive your death. Therefore, if you include items in your will that you have already disposed of in your prenuptial agreement, you are risking a lawsuit between your spouse and the recipients of the items you name in your will.

There is some confusion among the public about the strength and validity of prenuptial agreements. Stories abound about how the agreements don't stand up in court. This becomes a concern in the context of estates because of the fear that the surviving party will try to overturn the prenuptial agreement to get more of the estate. In fact, prenuptial agreements are held to be valid except in certain specific circumstances.

One of the parties to the agreement could have the agreement overturned if that party could show that what he or she was getting under the agreement was outrageously unfair, and that he or she did not sign the agreement with the help of a lawyer. In the vast majority of cases, the parties do use lawyers to negotiate their agreements and help them sign them, so they are not able to later claim that the agreements were unfair or that they did not know what they were signing.

H. Matrimonial home

The home in which you and your spouse live, your "matrimonial home", may receive different treatment under the law than other pieces of real estate. This is to ensure that families don't suddenly find themselves either homeless or tied up in estate paperwork when one of the spouses passes away.

Each province has rules that apply to the matrimonial home that need to be taken into consideration when you are doing your planning. Many a parent has tried to leave his or her home to the children of a first marriage only to find that the home must go to the spouse of the second marriage regardless of what the will says. In many other cases, a husband or wife has deliberately kept the title to the family home in his or her name only when re-marrying, in the belief that doing so will ensure that the new spouse does not have any rights to the home. The reality is that there may be specific laws in place that prevent you from freely giving away your home in your will, even if your home is in your name only.

The rules vary widely from province to province. The following table shows how each province deals with the matrimonial home on the death of one of the spouses. Be sure to check for your province or territory to ensure that you know how your home will affect your estate planning puzzle. Remember to confirm this information when you see your estate planning lawyer.

Table 4: *Treatment of the matrimonial home when one spouse dies, according to province and territory*

Province or territory	What happens to the matrimonial home when one spouse dies and there is no will leaving the home to the surviving spouse and no joint title?
Alberta	If the spouse whose name is on the house dies, the surviving spouse can live in the matrimonial home for 90 days at the estate's cost but title doesn't transfer to the surviving spouse. Applies to married couples and adult interdependent partners (i.e. living together for at least 3 years).
British Columbia	When the spouse whose name is on the property dies, the surviving spouse has 180 days from the grant of probate to claim the matrimonial home. During that time, the executor can only sell the house without the spouse's permission if the rest of the estate is not enough to pay all of the debts of the deceased. If

	the spouse lives in the home during that time, he or she has to pay all of the costs of the home, including property taxes. After proper notice, the spouse may purchase the deceased's share of the home from the estate, using his or her share of the estate. If the value of the deceased's share of the home is more than what the spouse would get under the estate, the rest of the funds have to be raised by the spouse (using savings, mortgage, loan, etc.) The surviving spouse can apply to the court to have the house transferred to him or her without purchase under certain circumstances.

Manitoba	When the spouse whose name is on the property dies, the surviving spouse or common-law partner can live in the matrimonial home for the rest of his or her life but the title to the property does not pass to that surviving person. If the matrimonial home is a farm, the right includes the house itself and up to 320 acres of land. To qualify as a common-law partner for this purpose, the couple must have either registered their relationship or they must have cohabited in a conjugal relationship for at least 3 years.
New Brunswick	When the spouse whose name is on the title to the house dies, the surviving spouse does not have an automatic right to continue to live in the house, but he/she can ask the court to allow him/her to live in the property for the rest of his/her life,.
Newfoundland &	If the spouse whose name

Labrador	is on the house dies, the property is treated as jointly owned if the couple is legally married, so the surviving spouse gets the title to the house. If a common law spouse dies and his or her name was the only one on the title, the surviving common law spouse has no right of any kind to the property.
Northwest Territories	The surviving spouse may live in the matrimonial home for 60 days after the death of the spouse who owns the property, but title to the home does not transfer to the surviving spouse.
Nova Scotia	The surviving spouse can ask the court to allow him or her to live in the property for the rest of his or her life, even though the surviving spouse's name is not on the house. Title to the home does not transfer to the surviving spouse.

Nunavut	The surviving spouse may live in the matrimonial home for 60 days after the death of the spouse who owns the property, but title to the home does not transfer to the surviving spouse.
Ontario	The matrimonial home is treated like any other property so whoever is on the title keeps the house, unless otherwise ordered by a judge. If the house is left to someone other than the spouse in a will, the spouse (married) can stay there for 60 days at estate expense.
Prince Edward Island	When the spouse whose name is on the title to the home dies, there is no automatic right for the other spouse to own the home, but he/she can ask the court for an order granting possession of the house.

Quebec	When one spouse dies, the estate manages the assets of the deceased spouse, and the surviving spouse keeps his or her own assets. The surviving spouse is entitled to claim a division of the family property (called the "family patrimony"), including the house regardless of which spouse's name is on the title to the house. This applies only to married spouses and no common law spouses.
Saskatchewan	A surviving spouse has 6 months from the issue of Probate or of Letters of Administration to apply to the court for a division of family property.
Yukon	If the house is in the name of one spouse alone, and that spouse dies, the other spouse does not automatically obtain a half interest in the home.

A fact that may affect your planning is that any special rights to the matrimonial home as described in this table can legally be waived in writing by the person whose name is not on the title. They can agree not to claim the home or anything in place of the home. This can make a huge difference to what you have available to leave to your children, since a house is often one of the largest assets in a person's estate. For example, a man marries his fiancée, who lives in the home that she inherited from her parents. He moves in with her and the house is now their matrimonial home. They live in a province in which the spouse whose name is not on the property automatically receives the home. Because she wants the home to stay in her family and does not want to take the chance that he would inherit the house and pass it to his family, he signs a waiver of any rights he might have to the house. Once he has signed that waiver, she can give the house to whomever she wishes in her will. If he does not sign the waiver, he will inherit the house.

CHAPTER 6: TRUSTS

Trusts sound much more complicated than they really are, so don't automatically shy away from the idea of having a trust in your will. When properly drafted, they can be immensely useful in achieving estate planning goals. In this chapter, you will learn about "testamentary" trusts, that is, the kind of trust that is set up in your will, and some of the ways trusts are used. There are other types of trusts that you can set up during your lifetime, but their usage is not nearly as widespread as the use of testamentary trusts, so we will limit our discussion to the popular testamentary trusts.

A trust is a legal arrangement in which one person holds onto money or property for someone else's benefit. Once you start with that basic principle, you then flesh out the details such as describing exactly what property is being held, and for whom, and for how long. There are several legal and tax rules that arise when a trust is created, so every word of a trust must be carefully chosen. It's never a good idea to try to write your own trust in your will, but it is a good idea to understand how they can be used so that if your lawyer brings up the idea, you have an understanding of what he or she is talking about.

Below, some of the ways in which trusts are frequently used in wills in Canada are discussed. By reading these examples, you will see that trusts are very flexible instruments that can be tailored to your needs and goals.

A. Minor children

Children who are under the age of majority cannot legally accept their inheritance when that inheritance is money. While a child could possibly be given certain mementos or personal items, he or she could not be given money. This means that if a child is left an inheritance, it must be held in trust until the child is old enough to receive it. If you don't specify otherwise in your will, your child will receive a cheque for the entire amount of their inheritance on the day they come of age.

Many parents believe that receiving a sum of money, particularly a large sum, on their 18th or 19th birthday is not the best path for their children, as they wonder whether children of that age are mature enough to deal with the windfall. The larger the inheritance, the more parents worry about the possible effects. They are concerned that the child might fritter the money away foolishly, or be taken advantage of by unscrupulous people, or even that the child might lose incentive to work or gain an education.

This is where trusts can be extremely useful. Parents can use their wills to control several variables so that the children are protected and helped, rather than overwhelmed. If you were to go to an estate planning lawyer and state your goal of helping your children make their inheritance last and use it wisely, the lawyer would then be able to draft a trust that would help you attain those goals. While every case is unique, some of the variables that should be addressed in your will are discussed below.

i. The age of inheritance

In your will, you would state the age at which your child should inherit from you. Though it cannot be younger than the age of majority, it can be older. You can pick any age that you think is appropriate, though of course you should resist the temptation to try to control from the grave. Many parents choose an age in the late 20s, on the theory that the child will be mature by then, and will likely be in the stage of life where he or she could really use the money because he or she is thinking of marrying and perhaps buying a home.

You do not need to pick one age. You may state that the inheritance is to be given to the child in stages. Here are some examples:
- the child will inherit ¼ of his or her share at age 18, ¼ at age 22, ¼ at age 25, and the rest at age 28.
- the child will inherit in two equal parts, to be given out at age 25 and 30.
- the child will inherit 1/10th of his or her share a year for 10 years.

The options are almost endless. When deciding on an appropriate age to inherit, try to think about what your child might be doing with his or her life at that age. This is really difficult when your children are very young, but works well when your children are teenagers. For example, you may know by then that your children plan to attend university or college, which means not only that they probably won't have a paycheque for a few years, but also that they'll have large expenses for tuition.

These considerations about age also apply to grandparents who wish to set up trusts for their grandchildren.

ii. Encroachment

Encroachment refers to the ability to use some of the money for the child before the child is old enough to inherit. This important consideration is overlooked in many wills, but it's such a practical tool that it should always be discussed even if you ultimately decide against using it.

The logistics of encroachment are that the guardian who has custody of your child after you pass away would approach the trustee looking after your child's money. The guardian would express a need for funds, such as for braces for the child, tuition, hockey lessons, or a school trip. It could also be that the guardian approaches the trustee with a budget showing that there is a shortfall in the funds needed to properly care for the child on a regular basis. The trustee has the responsibility of saying "yes" or "no" to any request for funds. It is up to you, through your will, to say in advance what kind of thing the trustee can pay for. The will is your trustee's guide. The money is not paid to your child, but is paid to others on behalf of your child.

As stated a number of times, you need to have a clear goal in mind when you set up the trust for your children. If your goal is to ensure that your children live as comfortably as possible, you would most likely want a trust with a generous encroachment. If you wanted to make sure that your trustee did not overindulge the children and, as a result, have nothing left for the children when they come of age, you would probably have a somewhat more restrictive trust. For example, many parents say that they would be comfortable with the trustee purchasing a car for their child to attend university, but not if the car was a Ferrari. They are relying on the trustee to use common sense and maturity to assist a child who perhaps hasn't attained those qualities yet. You use your will to communicate to your trustee how you want them to deal with your children and their trust funds.

The most commonly-used encroachment clause says that the trustee may use the funds for any purpose for the "maintenance, education, and benefit" of the child. This is the widest discretion possible because it puts no restrictions on the type of expenses that could be covered. That particular combination of words covers everything from daily living expenses to emergency funds, and almost anything in between. Other parents opt for a more conservative clause that allows payment for medical emergencies only or for education expenses only.

When thinking about whether or not to include an encroachment clause, think about the reality of your children going to live with the guardians. The situation very much depends on the specifics of your case. One scenario is that you have only one child and the guardians are wealthy and have one child of their own. A very different scenario is that you have four children who would go into a family that already has three children of their own. Even in a well-off family, seven children is a lot to feed, clothe, educate, and take on summer vacation. In other words, you need to think of the financial strain you're putting on the guardians, and whether you are able to help the situation (and your child's standard of living) by encroaching on your children's inheritance. Your guiding principle should be doing whatever is best for your children, taking all reasonable circumstances into consideration.

Trusts set up by grandparents for their grandchildren tend to be more restrictive in the use of funds. This is because many grandparents want to set up a trust for a specific purpose, such as helping with the cost of their grandchild's education. While parents are ultimately responsible for supporting their children's day-to-day needs, grandparents are not. Grandparents can simply leave a gift, not because they have to but because they want to. They may feel more free to choose to support only one specific goal such as education or medical needs, since presumably the child's parents are looking after the basics.

Not all parents choose to allow an encroachment on funds. It's not required by law. This is something that each parent must decide when planning his or her will. The decision will be based on the variables discussed above, as well as the practical matter of how much money is available. If the inheritance is not a large one, you might feel that is should be put aside, invested, and allowed to grow as much as possible, then given to the child when he or she comes of age.

Another important factor is the number of years left before your child reaches the age of majority. If your child is already quite close to becoming an adult, there is less need to create a trust that will accommodate every possible childhood need.

Assuming that you like the idea of allowing encroachment on trust funds, try to ensure that the lawyer tailors your will to reflect your wishes. You can get quite detailed, if that is what works best. For example, let's say that in your will you have directed your executor to set aside a trust for your child, and the child will receive it at age 22. You think it's a good idea to use an encroachment. Your child will be going to university, and so you set up something like this:

- While the child is going to post-secondary school (and attaining passing grades), the trust may be accessed to pay her tuition, books, and supplies;
- Your trustee has the final discretion to decide what qualifies as a post-secondary institution, but you want it wide open so that your child can attend university, college, trade school, or any school that teaches her a practical skill, profession, or trade;
- While the child is in university and living with the guardian, your trustee will pay the sum of $500 a month to the guardian to offset the cost of your child's food, clothing, etc.;
- If the child is not living with the guardian while attending school – perhaps because she goes to a university out of the province, or lives in campus housing – then the $500 is paid to the child rather than to the guardian;
- If the child continues to live with the guardian once she has graduated from school but hasn't yet reached the age of 22 and so has not yet inherited, the trust will continue to pay the $500 per month to the guardian.

As you can see, this example is very detailed. Not all trusts are written to this level of detail, but that depends on what the parents want in their wills. A skilled wills lawyer can translate your wishes into a workable trust that will reflect your wishes. The advantage to using a trust with this level of detail is that you can cover many potential situations and provide real guidance to your trustee as to how you want things handled. The downside is that if the trust is not very carefully drawn, it might contain unintended contradictions.

iii. Choice of trustee

Another very important element of your child's trust is the choice of trustee. The trustee's main role is to look after the funds, invest them properly, and pay them out to the beneficiaries (your children) according to the terms of the will. Along with that, there are additional tasks such as completing tax returns for the trust. The trustee's most important job, however, is to use his or her discretion and judgement for each and every proposed payment. Your choice of trustee will impact how well the trust works.

Unless you say otherwise in your will, the trustee of your children's inheritance is the person you have named as executor of the will. Many people assume that the guardian they choose for the children is also the trustee, and in fact a few old-fashioned wills are still worded that way, but generally it is not the case. The two roles are actually very different. The *guardian's* job is to decide where the children live, with whom they live, and to stand in for the parents in daily life in matters such as the children's education, emotional development, and health. The *trustee's* job is strictly to look after the money and pay the bills, and the trustee has no say in how or where the children live.

If you don't want your executor to be the trustee of your children's trust, then you need to appoint a trustee in your will.

When choosing the person or people who will look after your child's inheritance, your first criterion is going to be trustworthiness. Obviously you want someone honest who is not likely to embezzle your child's funds. Ideally you would have a candidate in mind who is also good with money, smart, compassionate, geographically close by, and who shares your values about things such as education. Not everyone who makes a will has access to that bundle of qualities in one person who is also willing to be a trustee.

Use common sense when choosing a trustee, and try to keep emotional factors to a minimum. That is not always easy to do, if you feel that you should choose a specific person out of loyalty or obligation, or if you don't want to hurt their feelings. Try to put those feelings aside and think of the trusteeship as a job you need to fill. Think of the requirements discussed above and try to find a person who embodies them. Sometimes when loyalties and emotions lead the way, people end up making poor choices. For example, sometimes individuals choose their sibling as trustee because they don't want to offend or upset that sibling by choosing someone unrelated. That doesn't work out well if the sibling has a gambling problem, or has constant money pressures due to chronic unemployment, or has other issues that make it a bad idea to give him or her access to a lot of unsupervised money.

Ask yourself whether it's better to risk hurting your sibling's feelings, or to risk losing your children's entire inheritance.

If you find that you have a very good option for someone to be the executor of your estate, but there is someone else you think would be a good trustee for your child's inheritance, you are able to set your will up that way. You are not required to have only one person. Different people have different skill sets and can be appointed to do different jobs. You have the choice of naming someone whose only job is looking after your child's funds, while someone else deals with the rest of the estate. This is done in your will by naming the trustee you want.

You may be considering naming the person who is your child's guardian to be the trustee as well. In other words, there would be just one person in charge of both the child's upbringing and the child's inheritance. There are two schools of thought on whether that's a good idea. On one hand, you might think that if you trust someone enough to task them with the physical and emotional care of your child, you are okay with letting them handle the money as well. If that is your mindset, you will likely have the same person act as guardian of the children and trustee of their funds, as that is the simplest arrangement.

The opposing school of thought is that it's a good idea to have more than one set of eyes on money that belongs to children who are too young to know what's going on financially. Sometimes funds belonging to children go missing or are outright stolen, and sometimes they are just sloppily managed. Ultimately, the choice will depend on your relationship with the person you are naming as guardian, and what you perceive to be that person's strengths and limitations. Of course, your choice may also depend on who else is available to you. Not everyone has a large, extended family from whom to choose their representatives.

If you don't have family members who you think should be handling your child's inheritance, you may have to look further afield. A good option for those who are leaving a large sum of money (say, $100,000 or more) in trust is to consider using a trust company. You may choose to name the trust company as your executor, but as mentioned above, your executor and trustee do not have to be the same person. As an example, you could name your affectionate, nurturing sister as the guardian of your children, your businesslike brother as the executor of your general estate, and a trust company as the trustee of the child's inheritance.

A discussion with your estate planning lawyer should help you sort out the pros and cons of your choices. Also keep in mind that you can have a no-obligation chat with the trust company representatives if you just want to find out more about how they would work for your child, or what it would cost.

B. Disabled child

An adult who is physically disabled is not necessarily likely to need a trust. For most people, a physical disability does not cause the individual to require help with money management, though of course each person is unique. Technology will generally assist a physically disabled person carry out the tasks that he or she needs to do. An individual in that situation may not appreciate having someone make financial decisions for them based on mobility issues. However, a mental disability is sometimes another story. A trust is used when an adult has a mental disability that prevents him or her from being able to handle property and money in a reasonable way.

The parents of a child with a mental challenge often want to set up their wills in a way that will help a mentally disabled child with their inheritance once the child has reached adulthood. The parents want to be sure that the money is invested wisely and being spent in a way that will make it last as long as possible to support the child. They also want to ensure that the child is not taken advantage of. The tool used to achieve these goals is usually a trust in the parents' wills.

As with any trust, the parents will determine the goals of the trust, such as:
- How much money is to be put into trust;
- How long it should stay in trust (generally speaking, a trust for a mentally challenged person is held in trust for his or her entire life);
- Exactly who may receive money from the trust;
- What the money is to be used for;
- Who the trustee will be;
- How much discretion the trustee has to grant or refuse requests for money from the trust; and
- Who receives the money at the end of the trust, after the disabled person has passed away.

There is one specific issue that arises when the beneficiary of a will is a disabled person and many families should plan around it. The disabled person is probably receiving a disability benefit from the province in which he or she lives. The benefit is usually a monthly sum of money as well as access to free medical, dental, and optical care. The issue arises because of the rules that apply when a person receives those provincial benefits. The rules restrict both the amount of assets a disabled person may own and the amount of income he or she may earn. Those who have more than the allowed amount are cut off from the valuable provincial benefits. If the disabled person inherits money or property, he or she risks losing the provincial benefits even though the inheritance is not large enough to support the person for the rest of his or her life. Once the inheritance is used up, the disabled person is once again required to go through the assessment steps to try to receive the government benefits.

To address this issue, lawyers use a specific type of trust known as a "Henson Trust". It's effective everywhere in Canada other than Alberta.

The key characteristic of a Henson Trust is that the trust is discretionary. This means that the trust is written so that the trustee of the trust has the ability to pay some or all of the money to the disabled person, but is not legally required to pay the person anything. And if the trustee is going to pay some money, he or she has full power to decide how much will be paid and when it will be paid. The disabled person cannot insist on receiving any funds as the trustee has total control. Because of this discretion given to the trustee, the disabled person cannot be said to own the money in the trust, since he or she might never actually get a cent of it. Therefore, the disabled person is not forced to give up provincial benefits.

A parent who is going to leave millions of dollars to a disabled child is perhaps less concerned about whether or not their child is eligible for provincial benefits. With that much money available in trust for the child, the child has enough to live on for life already, and outside benefits become less crucial. However, for parents who are leaving a more modest amount for their children, it is often important to set up a trust that does not interfere with those valuable benefits.

C. Spendthrift

On occasion, a parent wants to set up a trust for a child in order to protect that child from himself or herself. This is usually because the child is extravagant with money and the parent believes that the child will "blow" the inheritance very quickly. In other cases, they feel that their child is simply too easily taken advantage of by their friends, romantic partners, or other people. A trust that is set up to handle money for someone who is not mentally disabled and is not a minor, but needs some help managing money, is sometimes called a "spendthrift trust". Its purpose is to put someone else in charge of the money so that it is handled in a more responsible way.

If you are planning to use this kind of trust, be aware that it won't necessarily be obvious to the beneficiary or to your executor why you set up this trust. You are not required to explain your decision to use a trust, as it is your money and you are entitled to choose how you give it away. However, when beneficiaries don't know why their share is being held in trust, they sometimes feel they are being punished or unnecessarily restricted. Sometimes they even go to court to try to get the trust dissolved so they can have their inheritance right away. They are not always successful, of course, but should they take your estate to court, everything is delayed while your executor responds to the lawsuit, and this may also result in extra legal fees for your estate.

A few words of explanation can go a long way. You do not have to give a long, detailed description. You don't have to hurt anyone's feelings. However, you could add a line to your will that says that your intention is to allow your trustee to help the beneficiary make the money last as long as possible, or that you believe the beneficiary could use some support making financial decisions based on his or her history. You might also consider writing a Memorandum to Executor with an explanation of why you have set up the trust.

D. Creditor protection

While protecting an intended inheritance from creditors is not usually the primary goal when setting up a trust for a beneficiary, it is a useful side effect. When a beneficiary's share of an estate is placed in a trust, it is not owned by the beneficiary. Therefore if the beneficiary owes money, the funds in the trust cannot be accessed by the creditors. The only part of a trust that a creditor could seize is any part that is actually paid out to the beneficiary. In a discretionary trust (that is, one in which there are no regular payments and money only goes to the beneficiary when the trustee says so), the beneficiary may ask the trustee not to pay him or her anything while the debt is outstanding.

If creditor protection is a goal, it might be because the beneficiary is involved in business ventures and the testator wants to ensure that the beneficiary's share of the estate is not lost in the event that there is a business failure.

It's important to note, however, that trusts are not a way of avoiding paying an inheritance to someone who is in bankruptcy. If you become entitled to an inheritance while you are in bankruptcy, the executor is required by law to pay your entire inheritance to the bankruptcy trustee. The bankruptcy trustee will then use as much (or all) of your inheritance as is needed to cover your debt, and pay any unused amount to you. You cannot ask the executor to put it into a trust to protect it once you've inherited it, though this is routinely requested by beneficiaries in bankruptcy. The executor does not have the legal authority to create a trust to hold funds that were left directly to you in order to avoid bankruptcy, and in fact could be charged with fraud for doing so. The trust that protects a bankrupt's inheritance must have been set up by the deceased by including it in his or her will before he or she passed away.

If your inheritance was in a discretionary trust because the will directed that arrangement to be made, there is a good possibility that your inheritance would be protected from bankruptcy, but that depends on the circumstances and terms of the trust.

E. Blended families

These days, blended families of all kinds are very common, and estate planners have responded to these changing family dynamics with new tools. They've also found creative ways to apply the old standby – trusts. Trusts are very useful in estate planning for blended families because they allow you to control what happens to certain assets in the future. You can use a trust to allow someone to use an asset for a specific amount of time, then hand it on to the final beneficiary at a later date.

A very popular example of this use of trusts involves the family home. Let's say two people marry and move into the home that is owned by one of them. The owner of the home – Diana – is in her second marriage and has adult children from her first relationship. She wants one day to pass on her estate to those children, and her house is a large part of her estate.

At the same time, Diana wants to be fair to her husband, Marc. She would like him to be able to stay in their home for the rest of his life. However, she doesn't want to give him the house outright because she wants to be sure that her children eventually get it. If she leaves it outright to Marc, he could remarry and leave it to a new spouse. Or he could make a will that leaves it to his own children. Or he could sell it and spend the money, leaving nothing left over for Diana's children.

To manage all of her obligations and wishes, Diana may choose to use a trust. In her will, she could place her home, and possibly other assets, in a trust that would allow Marc to live in the home for the rest of his life without ever transferring ownership of it to him. The trust would state that on Marc's death, the title to the home would transfer to Diana's children.

A trust such as this is very effective, but it must be set up so that it does not contradict anything that Diana and Marc have agreed to in a pre-nuptial or cohabitation agreement. It must also work with any Memorandum of Personal Effects that Diana might have made to deal with the contents of the home. In addition, it should be considered in the context of Dependent's Relief laws as discussed in chapter 1 of this book. Remember that your estate plan is like a puzzle that you put together with all of the right pieces fitting each other.

Although this example specifically discusses holding a house in trust, trusts are frequently set up with a range of assets such as life insurance proceeds or investment portfolios. In some cases, a husband or wife might leave the entire estate in trust. The choice of what to leave in trust should be made after a thorough discussion of the assets of the couple as well as their goals and challenges. Holding a home in trust might not work if the spouse living there has no source of income to maintain the home or to pay for insurance or taxes. Using a trust is a great idea as long as it is set up realistically.

If you are interested in setting up a trust to hold a house for future owners while allowing someone else to live there, here are some of the questions that would have to be answered in the trust itself:

- How long can the person live there?
- Can anyone else move in, such as a new spouse or common law partner?
- What happens to the furniture and décor items in the house? Are they held in trust too?
- What if the occupant can no longer afford to live in the house?

- Can the occupant ask that the house be sold and a new one be bought to replace it?
- If the occupant moves out for a while, can the trustee assume that the occupant has abandoned the house?
- Who is paying for keeping the house in good repair?
- Who is paying for property tax and insurance?
- Who is paying for consumable items such as heat, water, light, internet, telephone, and TV?
- Can the occupant rent out part of the house, or the whole house?
- What happens if the occupant fails to pay the items that are his or her responsibility?
- Once the occupant moves out, what happens to the house?

Any time you are considering setting up a trust for your partner or spouse, you must take the time to think it through, and, ideally, talk it through with the person who is going to live there. Work through all the details to see whether your idea is workable, and to determine whether there is anything in particular you must include in your trust to protect the house, your spouse, and the people who will inherit the house once your spouse moves out.

F. Income splitting

A trust is a separate entity from the people who put money into it (the "settlors"), the people who look after that money (the "trustees") and the people who will one day receive that money (the "beneficiaries"). Because the trust is itself an entity, it is a tax-payer. This means that a trust can earn income just as an individual can and a trust must file income tax returns annually to deal with its income.

This aspect of the trust entity makes it a useful tool for families who are already paying high income taxes and want to avoid incurring any more tax than is necessary.

For example, Max and Rolenda are a married couple. Rolenda owns about $5 million worth of assets of her own, and makes a good salary as well. As a result, she pays high taxes. Max has significant assets as well, so when he makes his will, rather than leaving all of his assets to his wife, Max leaves a large chunk of his estate to a trust. The trust under Max's will names only Rolenda as a beneficiary and she can access the assets any time she wants.

Then, when Max passes away, Rolenda does not inherit a lot of money as most of Max's assets go into the trust. The interest that is earned on the money in the trust, instead of going to Rolenda, stays in the trust. Rolenda's income doesn't increase and her tax situation is not affected. The trustee does an annual tax return for the trust that accounts for all of the income on Max's assets. There are now two tax-payers – Rolenda and the trust – paying taxes rather than just Rolenda.

G. Keeping the inheritance away from the in-laws

A large number of parents who are making wills specifically request that their children receive their inheritance in such a way that the children's spouses cannot get access to it in the event the child passes away. This request generally arises from a concern that if their child should die, the child's spouse will inherit the estate, re-marry, and then leave the estate to the new spouse. The fear is that the grandchildren may not receive anything from the estate. In other cases, the parents simply do not approve of their child's choice of spouse.

Even where there are no grandchildren, parents often express a concern about the inheritance they intend to leave their children eventually ending up in the hands of their children's spouses. Parents also worry that if they leave an inheritance to their child, and the child later divorces, the child's spouse will walk away with half of the inheritance.

This is not at all unusual and parents should not feel uncomfortable about wanting to ensure that their child's inheritance is protected from his or her spouse. In fact, intestacy laws across Canada are built on a system that follows the bloodlines of families and by-passes the in-laws entirely. When individuals pass away without leaving wills, any share that was to go to their children would be divided among the deceased child's children. While an individual cannot easily leave his or her own spouse out of his or her will, there is absolutely no obligation – or generally speaking, any expectation - to give anything to the spouses of their children.

A trust is a handy tool that can answer these concerns. A popular way to set out the arrangement in a will is as follows:
- The parents leave a share of their estate to their child in their will;
- The parents' wills then state that if a child dies before the parents, the child's children (the grandchildren of the parents) divide up the

deceased child's share;
- If a grandchild is a minor when the grandparent dies, the grandchild's share is held in trust according to the terms of the grandparent's will;
- The trustee of the grandparent's will looks after the grandchild's money.

As you can see, the funds that the child would have received if he or she had not passed away will never pass through the hands of the child's spouse. In fact, some parents request that the will contain a specific restriction preventing the trustee from ever placing any of the grandchild's funds in the care of the deceased's child's spouse under any circumstances.

Keep in mind that if your child inherits from you and puts the inheritance into an asset that he or she shares with his or her spouse, the matter is a little bit more complicated. You cannot prevent your child from receiving funds from the trust and buying a gift for his or her spouse, or spending the inheritance on something that they own jointly.

CHAPTER 7: TAXATION

Taxation is one of the toughest areas of estate planning to work with. Perhaps that's why so many individuals simply don't think about or talk about tax issues during the estate planning process. Ignoring tax issues is not a good idea. As has been mentioned several times in this book, you should expect this issue to be raised by your estate planning lawyer, as everyone should be aware of the possible tax consequences of his or her estate plan. A lawyer is not an accountant, but your lawyer should be able to alert you to possible tax issues and, if necessary, refer you to an accountant to get more personalized tax advice.

The majority of Canadians will find that their estates are going to be affected in one way or another by tax on their deaths. It's something that is inevitable, but proper planning can avoid unnecessary or extra tax, and can help you set up your financial affairs to minimize tax. Planning can also help you avoid surprises for your family that will disrupt the wishes set out in your will.

Contrary to popular belief, the federal government in Canada does not take a death tax when someone dies. There is no automatic percentage of your estate that goes to the federal government, despite persistent rumours to the contrary. There are two types of federal taxation that may affect your estate, and both are discussed in some detail in this chapter.

There is also a probate fee charged by the courts when an executor sends a will to probate. This is a provincial fee that varies quite a bit across the country. Because the fee is calculated according to the value of the estate, many people refer to this probate fee as a tax. In Ontario, it is actually called an estate administration tax but the rest of the country refers to it as a probate fee. This fee is also discussed in detail later in this chapter.

Another myth about taxation that can be dispelled is the one that says that the government will take a portion of your inheritance once you receive it. This is false. In Canada you can inherit from a Canadian estate without incurring any tax whatsoever on your inheritance.

This doesn't mean that the money you inherit is forever exempt from any tax. For example, if you inherit half a million dollars, you will receive it tax-free. But if you invest that money and earn interest on it, you will pay tax on the interest, just as you pay tax on the interest earned on any other money you invest.

As you read this chapter and learn more about how taxation of estates works in Canada, there is one tip that will help simplify the rules and concepts. Tax is levied against a *transaction* and not against an *asset*. This is an important distinction, and if you master it, it will help you immensely.

For example, let's say that a mother leaves her home to her son. Because it's her principal residence (more about that later), there is no tax when the house transfers from the mother to the son. Let's say the son lives in his own house with his family, but he holds onto his mother's house for a couple of years. When he sells it, if it has increased in value while he owned it, it will be taxed. The *asset* - that is, the house – is not taxable. However, the *transactions* – the transfer from mother to son and later from son to buyer – are subject to tax. Sometimes people are very surprised to find that a house that they thought was tax-free is suddenly taxable, because they mistakenly thought the tax status belonged to the house rather than the sale.

A. Capital gains tax

Capital gains tax is payable when you own certain assets, known as "capital assets" and you dispose of them at a value higher than the value for which you acquired them. Disposing of the assets can mean selling them, but it also refers to the assets leaving your possession because you have passed away.

The capital assets owned by most Canadians are homes, cabins, land, and shares of private companies. If you own any of these, you should consider whether they are likely to trigger tax liability in your estate when you pass away.

To get a ballpark estimate of what your capital gain liability might be, follow this formula:

1. Start with the fair market value of the asset now.
2. Subtract what you paid for it.
3. Subtract the amount you paid for improvements to the asset (e.g. new septic tank for the cabin, new roof, adding the deck, updating the electrical or plumbing).
4. The resulting number is the amount of your gain.
5. Cut that number in half. This number is the amount of income you will have to add to your tax return for the year you disposed of the property.

Example:
Jacob bought a cabin for $75,000. He spent $20,000 on improvements including installing new windows and a new roof. When he passed away, his cabin was worth $160,000.

Jacob's gain is calculated like this:

160,000	current market value
(75,000)	subtract what he paid for it
(20,000)	subtract value of improvements

65,000 is the amount of the capital gain.

Half of the gain is taxable so the gain is divided by two:
65,000 ÷ 2 = 32,500

Jacob's accountant will add $32,500 to the income declared by Jacob in his tax return.

Please note that this is an extremely simplified explanation designed to give you the broad strokes of this complex tax concept. There are dozens of rules and other details that are best left to accountants who specialize in tax. Executors should never complete the tax returns for the estate themselves unless they happen to be accountants or trained tax preparers. Using an accountant to do the final return for the deceased person as well as any returns for the estate itself is a legitimate expense for any executor to incur.

B. **The principal residence exemption**

As mentioned earlier, the capital gains tax applies to land and houses. However, there are certain exemptions to the rules that are important for those doing their planning to know about. The first is the "principal residence exemption". This rule means that when a person dies, his or her home may be sold or given to a beneficiary tax-free. There are some rules around the home, and qualifying as a principal residence means more than simply the fact that the deceased lived there. For most people, the rule works simply because they only own one property. It is somewhat more complicated when a deceased person had more than one residence, as the exemption will only apply to one property.

A property can be claimed as a principal residence if:
   a) It is a house, cottage, apartment, condo, trailer, or houseboat;
   b) You own it, either alone or with someone else;
   c) During the year, it was lived in by you, your spouse, your former spouse, your common law spouse, your former common law spouse, or one or more of your children; and
   d) You have designated it as your principal residence.

There is sometimes a question about how much land may be claimed as exempt as being part of a principal residence, particularly where the lot on which the house is located is an acreage or other rural property. Many people do not realize that there is a limit. The general rule is that a principal residence may have half a hectare, or 1.24 acres, of land with it. There are some exceptions to that rule that allow more land to be included with a principal residence, such as where you can show that you need more than the standard amount of land to use the home. An example might be where a cabin or cottage is situated on a waterfront lot, but at such a distance that more than

1.24 acres is needed to access the waterfront.

A married couple may have only one principal residence between them. If you own more than one property, you may wish to consider which of them you will designate as your principal residence based on the value and the size of the property.

C. Farm rollover

Another very useful method of dealing with capital gains tax is the farm rollover. This is a method of transferring a family farm from one generation to the next without incurring the capital gains tax that normally would attach to the sale of the land. If the tax were to be payable when the farm passed from the parents to the kids, this could quite possibly deplete the farm assets to the point where the farm was no longer viable. The farm rollover is a mechanism to help keep the farm assets together so that the family can continue to operate the farm.

There are rules about making the transfer of a farm into a qualifying rollover. It must be a working farm going from one person who farms to another person who is going to farm. The person receiving the farm can be a son or daughter, grandson or granddaughter, or another person who falls within the guidelines.

A farm rollover is something that is generally thought of, discussed, and planned out before the farming person passes away. Obviously it cannot be done unless there is a person in the family who is interested in carrying on with the farming, and that person may already be involved in the farm operations in some way. The rollover may take place while the original farmer is still alive, but could also be done by his or her executor if the rollover is not completed by the time the original farmer passes away.

The rollover itself generally includes just the land and farming operations. There may be other issues to be resolved as part of the transaction, such as the use of the family home if it forms part of the farm.

If you are a farmer and you are thinking of using this very useful procedure to hand your farm to a family member, don't delay in getting started. You will need to do some research and spend quite a bit of time working out the details with your family. In addition, you should make sure that your will states your intention to do the farm rollover and that it instructs your executor to finish the rollover if you pass away before it is done.

D. Personal lifetime capital gains exemption

As mentioned earlier in this chapter, shares in privately-owned businesses are also capital property and are subject to capital gains tax when the owner of the business passes away. However, business owners are also given a bit of a break when it comes to tax, in the form of a deduction called the "lifetime capital gains exemption". Everyone who owns a small business in Canada is allowed to incur up to $750,000 in capital gains tax on their shares of the business. This is a total amount for a lifetime, so sometimes a person uses up the exemption during their life if they have bought and sold businesses. However, for many business owners, the exemption can be used when they pass away to reduce or even eliminate the amount of capital gains tax payable.

There are some rules, of course. For the two years prior to the business owner's death, the shares must be owned by him or her personally, or by someone related to him. In addition, 90% of the assets of the business must have been used to carry on business in Canada.

Knowing about this exemption, and knowing whether you have used up your personal lifetime exemption should help you with planning your estate. If you determine that you are going to incur a huge capital gains tax liability on your death, you can take steps to reduce that liability, or to ensure that you'll have cash on hand to pay for it.

E. Income tax

The second type of tax that may affect your estate after you pass away is income tax. This arises on certain registered financial instruments such as Registered Retirement Savings Plans (RRSPs) and Registered Retirement Income Funds (RRIFs).

When you add money to your RRSP during your lifetime, it is sheltered income and you are not taxed on the amount you add to the RRSP. The plan is set up so that while you are earning wages, you can put money aside to save for your retirement. It reduces the amount of tax you pay during your high-earning years because it allows you to pay the tax when you take the money back out, presumably many years later when you are no longer earning wages. RRSPs are very popular among Canadians and many of us own these savings plans.

When you take money out of your RRSP or your RRIF, you pay income tax on the amount you take out. For most people, this works well as, after retirement, they take out a monthly amount to live on. The estate planning issue arises if you still own an RRSP or RRIF at the time you pass away. The law says that your RRSP or RRIF is fully cashed out at the time you die, and therefore the entire thing is taxable. This means your estate has to pay the income tax.

The tax impact for RRSPs and RRIFs can be as high as 50% of the money in the plan. So, for example, if you own an RRSP that holds $100,000 when you pass away, you could be hit with a tax bill of $50,000.

This makes a difference to your estate because it leaves less for you to give your beneficiaries. As mentioned at the beginning of this chapter, a huge number of people never consider the tax implications of their estates at all and therefore don't ever realize that their estates are going to be reduced by a large amount of tax.

If you have a spouse who outlives you, your RRSP or RRIF can be "rolled over" to your spouse. This means adding your RRSP or RRIF money to theirs. If it "rolls over", there is no tax payable at the time. No tax is payable on your money until either your spouse takes it out to live on, or your spouse dies.

The spousal rollover is a special arrangement that is intended to help a married couple keep their finances together when one of them dies. It is your choice whether or not your RRSP or RRIF goes to your spouse. Normally you would choose who is going to get your RRSP at the time you set up the plan at your bank. The banker will ask you who is to be the beneficiary of the plan, and that information is recorded right on the plan itself. This means that you do not have to mention the beneficiary in your will because the RRSP or RRIF will go directly to the beneficiary from the bank and not pass through your estate.

The designation of beneficiaries is not particularly well understood among consumers when it comes to RRSPs and RRIFs. They often name their children as beneficiaries of these plans, particularly parents who are divorced or widowed and no longer have a spouse they wish to name. It is perfectly legal to name your children as the beneficiaries of your RRSP or RRIF, but the funds do not roll over to them. When you pass away and the funds flow to your children, your estate will have to pay the income tax that arises.

The tax liability that arises from the RRSP or RRIF can be set off to some extent by way of charitable donations. Just as you receive a tax credit when you give to a charity during your lifetime, your estate can receive a credit for donations as well. Some individuals like the idea of giving more to charities to reduce their final tax bill.

F. Probate fee/tax

The provincial and territorial governments do not levy a tax against estates. However, if a will is sent to the court to go through the probate process, or someone applies to become the administrator of an estate in the absence of a will, there is a probate fee payable. The probate fee is based on the value of the probatable estate.

The "probatable estate" refers to the portion of your estate that is affected by the probate process. It will include all assets that are held in your name alone, but will not include:
- A. Assets that you own jointly with other people (unless the other joint owners are your children, in which case the assets ARE part of your estate); and
- B. Assets on which you have designated a direct beneficiary, such as life insurance policies, pension benefits, RRSPs, and RRIFs.

In Ontario, the provincial probate fee is referred to as an estate administration tax. You can read more about probate fees and see a chart that shows exactly what the probate court charges in each province and territory in chapter 10.

CHAPTER 8: TIPS FOR A BETTER WILL

In this chapter, we are going to look at a few specific topics that are sometimes overlooked when wills are prepared. A will that does not contain the various items discussed here would still be perfectly valid, but might not be as strong, versatile, or as helpful as it could otherwise be. Remember that the stronger your will, the better you support your executor, and the best chance you give your family to deal with your estate without problems.

The purpose of this chapter is to alert you to the fact that some of these items could be problematic for you or your family if they are not addressed, and to explain why you might want to raise these issues with your lawyer. Not everything in this chapter is suitable for everyone, but it is intended to be food for thought.

If you don't already have a will, you may want to jot down some ideas to make sure your lawyer covers everything you need when he or she makes your will. If you already have a will in place, you can use this chapter to review your current document to see whether it could perhaps be improved or updated.

A. Executor compensation

Most people know that executors can be paid for their work, effort, and time spent on the estate. What is not so clear is how much they may be paid. This is an area of contention in a large number of estates, but it's a dispute that is easily preventable.

You may state in your will how much your executor should be paid. Historically, including this provision has not been the norm. Older wills rarely said anything at all about paying the executor, but over the years the issue of how much to pay the executor has ended up in court thousands of times. Setting out clear instructions for executor compensation is becoming more and more common as it becomes clear to lawyers and the public alike that addressing compensation in the will heads off disputes.

When I discuss payment of executors with parents who are naming their children as executor, they ask whether it even needs to be said. In my view, it does. The assumptions made by the parents – usually that the child would refuse to be paid simply because they feel it is their duty to act as executor – may not be the same assumptions made by the children. If the will is silent on the issue of paying the executor, one child will think "if Dad didn't want me to be paid, he would have said so", while another will think, "if Dad wanted me to be paid, he would have said so". If both of these are your children and they are trying to sort out your will, there is now a possible area of conflict that could easily have been avoided by you in advance.

You have the choice of naming a dollar amount for your executor's wage or naming a percentage. Most people opt to use a percentage for the simple reason that they don't know how much will be in their estates when they pass away so naming a dollar amount that is suitable is rather tricky. If you decide to use a percentage, you should be aware that the allowable range for executors across Canada is between 1% and 5% of the value of the estate. The word "allowable" used here means that it is the normal range of pay, and that if the executor had to ask the court to set his or her fee, it would fall within that range, barring exceptional circumstances. This doesn't stop some executors from trying to get huge percentages, but generally such large awards are only made if the estate has been involved in a court battle, or other extremely complicated matters have been handled by the executor. Executors may also claim reasonable out-of-pocket expenses over and above the fee they may be paid.

You can choose where on the range of 1% to 5% you think your executor should land. The higher range should be reserved for complex estates that require an executor to wind up a business, carry on a farm, or sell multiple properties in other countries. There is no need for an executor to receive 5% of an estate when the estate contains only a house and an RRSP, though certainly plenty of executors try for the maximum even when it is not merited. Obviously you will not know exactly what will be in your estate when you pass away, but you should have some idea. If your affairs are already simple, they are likely to stay that way.

Naming the amount of your executor's compensation avoids disputes because the case law in Canada is quite clear that when an amount is stated in a will, that's what the executor is going to get, and he or she may not ask for more. Think of it as a contract where you offer a certain amount of money to someone to carry out a certain job. When the job is done, the person cannot then decide to ask for more money.

When something unexpected happens on an estate, such as a lawsuit, the executor is entitled to ask for more compensation as the original deal was simply to administer the estate, not to defend a lawsuit.

There is a process to be followed in order for an executor to claim his or her payment. When your executor has wound up the estate, he or she will prepare a set of financial records for the beneficiaries to review. One of the pages in that set of records will be his or her claim for compensation. If the will does not state how much the executor is to receive, he or she will have to ask the beneficiaries of the estate to approve of his or her request for compensation. This often involves the executor being put on the spot and being asked to defend each and every trip to check on the house and every hour put into the estate. The beneficiaries know that the executor's compensation comes out of their inheritance and are usually pretty reluctant to let it go.

If the executor and the beneficiaries are not able to agree on the amount of the compensation, the only recourse left is to ask the courts to set the proper amount. This causes delays while the parties wait for the court date, and pits the various parties against each other as each tries to weaken the others' cases. It also usually ends up in extra costs for the estate if the judge wants the executor's legal fees to be paid from the estate.

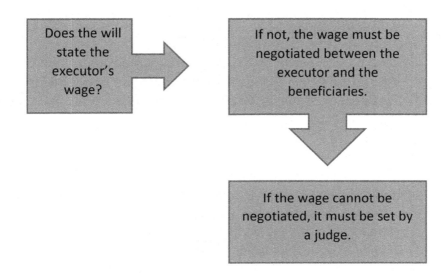

You can ensure that your family doesn't have to go through this particular argument by naming the amount of compensation in your will.

B. Public policy restrictions

There is a misconception among the public, supported by modern movies, TV shows and novels, that a will can express absolutely any wish that you want and that everyone has to do what you say. This is not quite true. The concept of putting anything you want in a will is known as "testamentary freedom" and refers to the idea that we all have the right to dispose of our hard-earned money as we wish. While in Canada we do enjoy testamentary freedom to a large extent, there are limits.

In this section, we are not talking about the limit imposed on testamentary freedom that is imposed by our obligation to support our legal dependents. That was covered in Chapter 1. Here we are talking about the idea that we would like to direct our beneficiaries to do certain actions in order to get their inheritance, or, as is more likely to be the case, to direct them *not* to do something in order to avoid losing their inheritance. While we do have a great deal of flexibility, the ability to put restrictions on inheritances in our own wills is not absolute.

There are restrictions based on what are known as "public policy" rules. These are rules that say you cannot do or say things in your will that go against the public good. For example, you cannot encourage someone to commit a crime in order to receive his or her inheritance, because crime is considered by the courts – and by most reasonable people - to be adverse to the good of society in general.

Another restriction that testators sometimes try to put into their wills is an instruction that an heir is not to receive anything from the estate if they should happen to get married. This is not a valid restriction; the courts will not uphold a will that discourages marriage, as restriction of marriage is seen as being adverse to society in general.

These are general rules and have for the most part been around for many, many years without being well known, but they tend to show up in real wills made by real people who are trying to work around something that bothers them. Recently the Canadian courts have dealt with cases that contained a gift that could be construed as racist. In one case, a testator left a gift to an organization whose stated purpose was to spread hate against an identifiable segment of society. In another case, a man set up his will to cut off a child for marrying a person of another race. In another case, a parent disinherited a child because the child was homosexual.

Cases like this sometimes end up in the courts because the executors are trying to figure out what they should do. They may bring the will to the judge and ask for direction on how to deal with it. However, in most cases this kind of will is contested by a beneficiary who is being cut out and wants the court to decide whether being cut out is fair.

These questions are always dealt with on a case-by-case basis. The facts of the case make a real difference in how the court rules. For example, in the will mentioned above in which a gift was being made to a racist organization, the court held that the gift to the organization was not valid. On the other hand, the court did uphold the will in which a parent cut out a child for racist reasons. The policy issues are not simple, since every policy that disallows a person from making the will they want chips away at our freedom to dispose of our own money the way we want. In the cases mentioned here, part of the reason the courts made the decisions they made is that a public organization should adhere to the Charter of Rights and Freedoms, in which we cannot discriminate based on race or religion. It seems as if the courts are more willing to allow a private gift (or lack of gift) than a public one.

If your will is contested on policy grounds, it will be wrapped up in the courts for many years, will lose thousands – if not tens of thousands – of dollars to legal fees, and will leave the beneficiaries sitting around waiting for money that they probably could have used. Therefore it is a good idea to exercise caution when trying to express an idea in a will that is generally not accepted by mainstream society. Discuss your goals with your estate planning lawyer to find out what your options are before going ahead.

If you have a certain wish or arrangement that you want to include in your will, it is a good idea to talk it over with an experienced lawyer first. If you include an unenforceable clause in your will, you risk the person who is being left out challenging your will. Once it ends up in court, it could be months or even years before any of your beneficiaries see their inheritances, and your estate will incur thousands of dollars in costs.

C. Contemplation of marriage

In some provinces, getting married automatically revokes any will you currently have in place. The way to avoid having your will revoked upon marriage is to use a clause that says your will is made in "contemplation of marriage". To do this, you state in your will the name of the person you intend to marry, and if you do actually marry that person, your will is not revoked.

For example, if Eldon had a will and later married his girlfriend, Maria Smith, the marriage would revoke Eldon's will. However, if Eldon's will contained a clause that said "I make this will in contemplation of marriage to Maria Smith", the marriage would not revoke his will. It's a very simple step that can prevent a lot of problems.

Using this clause is usually recommended to common law couples even though they have no immediate plans to marry. Generally, if a common law couple decides to marry in the future, they don't really think about the effect this has on their wills because the marriage isn't about that. They sometimes end up revoking their wills accidentally just by getting married. The revocation of their wills can be disastrous if their wills set up trusts for their children or made provisions for other family members.

This is not a general clause that allows you to marry an as-yet-unidentified person in the future without revoking your will. You have to name a specific person, and then marry that specific person in order for this clause to work. Note that including this clause in your will is not a proposal or a promise to marry anyone, and does not bind you legally.

Table 5: *Revocation of wills on marriage and divorce*

Province or territory	Is a will revoked on marriage?	Is a will revoked on divorce?
Alberta	No	No, but divorce will revoke gifts to the former spouse. Ending an adult interdependent relationship will revoke a gift to the adult interdependent partner.
British Columbia	No	No, but married spouses will be disinherited if: (i) the spouses live separate and apart for at least two years and at least one of them has the intention

		of living separate and apart permanently; or (ii) the spouses separate under the Family Law Act.
Manitoba	Yes	No, but divorce will revoke any gift in the will left to the former spouse. Divorce will revoke any appointment of the former spouse as executor.
New Brunswick	Yes	No, but divorce will revoke any gift in the will left to the former spouse. This does not apply to couples who are separated but not divorced.
Newfoundland & Labrador	Yes	No
Northwest Territories	Yes	No
Nova Scotia	Yes	No, but divorce will revoke any gift in the will left to the former spouse. Divorce will revoke any appointment of the former spouse as executor.

Nunavut	Yes	No.
Ontario	Yes	No, but divorce will revoke any gift in the will left to the former spouse. Divorce will revoke any appointment of the former spouse as executor.
Prince Edward Island	Yes	No, but divorce will revoke any gift in the will left to the former spouse. Divorce will revoke any appointment of the former spouse as executor.
Quebec	No	No, but divorce will revoke any gift in the will left to the former spouse. Divorce will revoke any appointment of the former spouse as executor.

Saskatchewan	No	No, but divorce will revoke any gift in the will left to the former spouse. Divorce will revoke any appointment of the former spouse as executor.
Yukon	Yes	No

D. Instructions for your remains

There is some debate among estate practitioners and their clients about whether or not your will is the appropriate place to leave instructions for your burial, cremation, memorial service, or other matters relating to your remains.

On one hand, it would seem a waste of time to put instructions of this sort into a document that most likely won't even be looked at until after you have been buried. Certainly the will is not the first consideration for most families who lose a loved one, and for that reason many lawyers don't consider your will the best place to leave that sort of instructions.

On the other hand, if the family should end up in a dispute about what to do about your remains – and plenty of families do - they are more than likely going to consult your will at some point to see if you said anything about it. Anything that may help to resolve a dispute is worth including.

If you wish to include some instructions in your will, keep in mind that your executor does not have to follow them. Though it may seem strange to include directions in a will that executors are allowed to ignore, this type of wish is an exception to the rule that the executors must follow your wishes. The legal term for an instruction in a will that is really just a wish because it isn't legally binding is "precatory". Executors have the legal responsibility to dispose of your body and therefore they also have the legal right to decide how that is to be done.

If the manner of disposal of your remains is important to you, make sure that you discuss it with the person you want to appoint as your executor. Hopefully your executor will accept your ideas and wishes. This has from time to time become a problem where the executor wants to take steps to deal with a body that are not in accordance with what the rest of the family wants to do. Holding a frank discussion will give you a good idea of whether your executor is wholeheartedly in favour of honouring your choices or whether he or she is reluctant.

Some of the more popular instructions that people choose to include in their wills are:
- Cremation
- Burial
- Scattering of ashes in a place chosen by the testator due to its sentimental appeal
- Ashes to be scattered in the discretion of the children
- Hold a celebration of life rather than a sad service
- Keep the service small and inexpensive
- Don't hold a viewing, or have viewing for family only

- Burial in a cemetery in a family plot
- Burial next to husband or wife
- Burial of ashes of a beloved pet with you
- Choice of which faith or religion should be observed
- Choice of hymns or other music for the service
- Choice of particular church, synagogue, or other place of worship

As you can see, there is quite a range of possible wishes. Some people go further and request parties for their friends. Some ask that there be no service or memorial of any kind. Now that new technologies are changing the way we dispose of remains, people are beginning to request that their ashes be pressed into "diamonds". Creative disposal of your remains is certainly an area in which you can express yourself.

E. Asking the impossible

Sometimes people give instructions in their wills that are simply impossible to implement. This happens frequently in home-made wills in which the testator did not think through how his or her wish would actually work.

For example, a person making his or her will might say that the beneficiary could not inherit unless he or she quit smoking, and if the beneficiary started smoking again within three years, the inheritance had to be repaid. This wish does not violate public policy (which was discussed earlier in this chapter) as encouraging someone to stop smoking does not harm society. However, it is impossible for an executor to carry out.

There are simply too many unanswered questions for this plan to be manageable. How is the executor to know for sure that the person has quit smoking? How long does a person have to not smoke before it qualifies as quitting? Does the executor personally have to monitor the person for the next three years? Does one cigarette in three years mean that the beneficiary has resumed smoking? And how would the executor compel the beneficiary to repay the money? What if the beneficiary no longer has the money? And if by some chance it was repaid to the estate, who inherits it then?

In other words, the concept is lawful, but the execution of it is not workable. Other clauses that are also problematic that have appeared in wills say that beneficiaries can inherit if they "have got their life together". Again, this is an impossible task for the executor to carry out because there is simply no way to measure or address the condition imposed in the will. How will the executor know whether the person has their life together? What does that even mean? Does it mean employed? Drug-free? In a stable relationship? Some combination of those? What would the executor have to do to find out about the quality of the person's life, especially if it isn't someone he or she knows?

There are some identifiable and measurable metrics than can be used in a will. For example, you can state that a person must have reached a certain age, attained a post-secondary degree, be a parent, or have a valid driver's license. These are facts that the executor can verify if necessary, and of course there are many other possibilities.

If you are thinking about leaving a gift in your will that depends on your beneficiary doing or not doing something in particular, be sure to talk through your idea with your lawyer first. If it is something that can be properly identified and measured, it might be possible, or there may be another way to attain the goal you wish to reach.

F. Where do you leave your estate if you have no family?

Not everyone has a spouse or children to whom they will leave their estates. Others have a spouse, but no children. Some people have no family members at all. Others have family members such as siblings and cousins but don't feel that those family members are in need of anything from their estates. Plenty of individuals in all of these situations are looking for ideas for where to leave their estates when they have passed on.

Below you will find a few ideas for those who do not have children, or for those who would prefer not to give their estates to their children. Not every idea will suit everyone, of course, but hopefully this list will get you thinking about possibilities. Some of these ideas require a large estate in order to carry them out, but most can be done with even a very modest estate.

i. Charitable Organizations

The simplest answer to the question is to leave something to a charitable organization. However, that simple answer conceals the variety of possibilities that are encompassed by the idea of leaving funds to a charity. You can be quite creative in choosing a recipient.

One idea is to choose a charitable organization – or several organizations - that supports a cause you care about, such as relief of poverty or research into cancer. Another idea is to choose an organization that supports a group that is important to you, such as homeless people or refugees. For ideas on where to give your donation and more information about the benefits of charitable giving through your will, check out websites such as www.leavealegacy.ca.

While giving funds to a charity is for many people its own reward, there is also a purely financial benefit to giving to a charitable organization in your will. Your estate will receive a deduction for the gift, thereby increasing the amount available for giving. For more on this topic, refer to Chapter 3 of this book.

ii.   Set up a Scholarship

A popular idea is to create a scholarship that would benefit one or more students. When setting up this type of bequest, you can make detailed choices to ensure your goals are attained. For example, you would choose a university or college, choose a faculty or program, and set the parameters for a student to receive the scholarship. For example, you could state that the student who wins the scholarship would be the one with the highest marks in math, or had financial need, or had already completed two years of the music program. You could specify graduate students or undergraduate, or which year of the program the candidate should be taking. These are very personal gifts in the sense that they can fulfill very detailed wishes that reflect your personal values.

Depending on the size of your donation, the scholarship could be a one-time event, but in most cases the capital of the gift is invested and only the interest earned on the investments is used to pay the scholarship. In that way, your gift could be given year after year for a long time to come, benefitting several students.

Scholarships generally carry the name of the person who created them, so you would be remembered by each student who won the scholarship.

iii. Create a foundation

Creating a foundation is similar to giving a charitable gift, but has one specific difference: it gives for many years, and possibly even forever (in legal terms, this is referred to as giving "in perpetuity").

The idea behind setting up a foundation is that the capital of the charitable gift is invested, and only the income from the gift is used to give to the charitable organizations named. The choice of recipients is almost endless, and a foundation can be set up to benefit one cause, or many. The choice is made by the individual who donates the funds.

Many foundations are created by wills of individuals who want or need to have all of their money available during their lifetimes, and want to fund their new foundation after they pass away. In this way, they have no set-up costs during their lives, and their money is not restricted in any way. A variation on this arrangement is that an individual can set up the foundation while alive, fund it in part with available money, then add the rest of the money to the foundation through the will when they pass away. They may choose to do this to obtain an annual charitable deduction that can be used to offset income tax. They may also enjoy the act of giving to the charities and seeing their foundation in action while they are alive.

Setting up a foundation from scratch can be expensive. If you're interested in learning more about this idea, be sure to consider your city's community foundation, as it may well already have an existing foundation to which you can donate. Some larger financial institutions also have existing foundations that are ready for you to add your donation, such as Scotiabank's Aqueduct Foundation.

iv. Political Parties

Canadians have been leaving donations to federal political parties through their wills for years. Living individuals are currently allowed to donate no more than $1,200 per year, but this limit does not apply to estates. In fact, there is no cap on the amount of funds you can leave to the registered political party of your choice in your will.

Like leaving a donation to the charity of your choice, leaving a donation to a political party can be an expression of your personal values.

v. Create a memorial

An environmentally friendly idea to use part of your estate is to sponsor a tree planting in your name. While strictly speaking a tree planted by your estate is really a memorial to you, the positive effects go beyond your family's memories and touch other members of your community.

Planting trees can beautify a city or park and help keep our environment clean.

Consider having a tree – or any number of trees – planted in your memory. In most places you would have to obtain permission from the city or town to plant on public land.

Another idea along the same lines is a memorial bench. This would be a public park bench bearing a small plaque stating that the bench was placed there by your family in your memory. You would be providing a place for someone to sit and admire a lovely view or read on a sunny day.

vi. A send-off by your friends

Though many people strongly believe that estate assets should be passed down to family, passing away without leaving children gives you the opportunity to leave a gift to friends. You can name any of your friends as beneficiaries, regardless of where they live, and can leave them any gift you like. Of course you can simply leave them a sum of money, but if you wanted to, you could be creative and you specify how they are to use the money.

A popular idea is to leave a sum of money that is enough to pay for your specified group of friends to hold a party in your memory, or even to take a vacation together to a particular place that has significance for the group. For example, if you and your friends are avid golfers, you could leave enough money for your group of friends to play a particular course in Scotland that you'd always wanted to visit but had not gotten around to during your lifetime.

vii. Sponsor an Olympic athlete

If you enjoy a specific sport, or wish to support athletes or physical fitness in general, it is possible to contribute financially to assist Canadians who are training for the Olympics and Paralympics. Donations would potentially fund an athlete's equipment, coaching, food, and travel expenses. Published statistics indicate that 80% of Canadian Olympic athletes rely on funding from donors.

There is an ongoing program that accepts donations from anyone who wishes to help out. Be sure to read the material on the websites thoroughly to understand how you can fit into the program and whether there are any restrictions or conditions that might apply to you.

viii. Build a museum

An individual's interest in creating a museum often begins with that person's passion that has led to a lifetime of collecting. Whether the collection is of movie memorabilia, antique cars, or the paintings of a particular artist, it may be a large enough group of items to form the beginning of a museum that will one day be available for the public to enjoy. Many people who collect items express a wish that the collection be kept together if at all possible. That's not easy to achieve if the estate is being split among several beneficiaries or if the collection is being sold.
Depending on the size of your estate, you may have adequate assets to purchase or lease a building and begin the display and interpretation of your collection. A variation of this idea is to donate your collection to an existing museum or library to add to its collection.

If you decide to set up your collection for public viewing, ensure that you leave careful, specific instructions for your executor in your will about the goals you want to achieve and your plans for reaching them. It's also a good idea to talk the idea out thoroughly with your lawyer and your financial advisor to ensure that you have considered all costs and expenses, as well as all local laws.

CHAPTER 9: GETTING ADVICE

As you no doubt have gathered while reading this book, putting together an estate plan is something that you are probably going to want help with. While of course it's possible to buy a will kit and simply make a will yourself, that doesn't suit everyone. A will kit is a useful and economical tool for someone whose financial and family affairs are extremely simple and straightforward. You may have realized after reading this book that your affairs are not quite as simple as you had thought, and that it's going to take more than a simple will to pull all the pieces together. You should not be using a will kit to prepare your will if:

- You are in a second or subsequent marriage;
- You are in a blended family;
- You own a business;
- You have a disabled child;
- You own a cabin, summer home, or rental property;
- You own property outside the country;
- You want to make an unequal distribution among your children;
- You have put any of your children's names on your assets;
- You have minor children;
- You have adult children who are pressuring you about your estate.

When individuals want help with their estate planning, there are three main sources of professional assistance. Those are the lawyer, the accountant, and the financial advisor. You may wish to call on all three, or perhaps you will only need to consult a drafting lawyer. In this chapter, you will gain a better idea of what to expect from each of those advisors in terms of your estate planning. Remember that if your estate is complex, you may have planning meetings in which all of your advisors attend together to ensure that all details are covered.

A. Lawyer

The lawyer is usually the first advisor people approach, and for many it's the only advisor they need to have their complete estate plan prepared. The lawyer will discuss your goals, your family, and your assets and will help you shape all of that into legal documents. Your lawyer should draft your will, your Enduring Power of Attorney, and your healthcare directive. These documents should *never* be prepared by your accountant or financial advisor.

If other advisors are needed, it is usually the lawyer who acts as the coordinator of all of the parties, simply because the lawyer is the one who will produce documents after the other advisors have given their input.

Individuals are sometimes reluctant to hire a lawyer to have wills prepared because they fear that they will be presented with a huge bill for fees. It is perfectly acceptable to call a few lawyers in your area to ask about fees, but it's a good idea to ask a few additional questions as well. Instead of simply asking what a lawyer charges to prepare a will, consider asking this set of questions:
- What will the cost be?
- Does the price include an Enduring Power of Attorney and healthcare directive, and if not, how

- much do those cost?
- How long will it take for the job to be done?
- How much of the lawyer's practice is wills and estates?

This set of questions is designed to give you more information about what you are actually going to get if you should choose to hire that law firm. Most lawyers who do a lot of wills can do them efficiently and have them prepared for you within a few working days. There is no acceptable reason for a client to wait months for a basic will to be prepared, though that certainly happens to many people. A lawyer who cannot find the time to draft a will for several months is too busy to handle your file and you are better off finding someone else.

Look around for a lawyer who will prepare your documents for a set price or package price. This will give you some certainty about what your bill is going to be. Again, lawyers who do many wills know what their bill is going to be and can quote you a set price in advance. Keep in mind, though, that if you demand several re-writes or keep changing your mind about what you want, you should expect to receive a higher bill simply because most lawyers bill for their time spent.

The price of wills varies widely based on the lawyer's experience, the size of the firm, the geographic location, and the complexity of the work you need done. Individuals who last had their wills done twenty or more years ago are often shocked to find that wills can no longer be prepared by lawyers for $100.

It is a mistake to think that the lowest price is necessarily the best deal, as a lawyer who is undercutting his or her own time that way may be using wills as a loss leader, that is, a way of getting you into the firm, possibly to purchase more expensive services, rather than simply charging what the will is actually worth. Your best option is always to use a lawyer that has done wills for a friend or family member of yours and is recommended to you by that person.

i. Will and Enduring Power of Attorney

If at all possible, find a lawyer who specializes in wills and estates law. In larger cities, there are entire firms devoted to this type of law. In most large firms there are departments or individual lawyers who specialize in this type of law and handle all of that kind of work for the firm. In smaller towns, it's not always possible to find someone who specializes, but try to find someone who at least has several years of experience with drafting wills.

If you are calling around to various law firms to try to find a lawyer who specializes in wills, there is a very effective and simple way to get the information you need. Most people will call the lawyer and ask if the lawyer does wills. The lawyer is entitled to say yes, even if he or she only drafts one or two wills a year. A much better question to ask is how much of the lawyer's practice is comprised of wills and estates. The answer to that question will give you a much more accurate idea of just how much wills experience the lawyer actually has.

You should expect input, information, and advice from your lawyer. If you are simply asked what you want without discussion or input from the lawyer, you are not being properly represented. It's important that you tell the lawyer your whole situation even if you think it might make you look bad in some way, and that the lawyer gives you recommendations based on your individual needs. You should have a chance to ask questions and discuss your ideas.

Once you have given your instructions to the lawyer, you should be provided with draft documents to review at home, and a chance to make amendments to those drafts. You should receive the drafts within a reasonable time, which of course is going to vary based on the lawyer's schedule and workload. However, any lawyer should be able to produce a draft will within a couple of weeks. If the lawyer has warned you that he or she is going to be in trial every day for the next month or that he or she is going on vacation, certainly you can take that into account. Otherwise you are entitled to receive your drafts fairly quickly.

Often, a husband and wife will get their wills done at the same time using the same lawyer. This is not a problem and is in fact a very common scenario. However, this creates certain obligations on the part of the lawyer. The lawyer cannot keep secrets between the husband and wife. For example, a husband and wife have wills made together, then a year later the wife comes back to the lawyer alone and wants a new will that is to be kept a secret from the husband. The lawyer cannot do that second will.

ii.   Pre-nuptial agreements

Another way that lawyers are involved in estate planning is by drafting pre-nuptial agreements. Popular opinion of pre-nuptial agreements is that they are designed to deal with divorce, and that they are really only used by rich people. Neither of those ideas is completely true.

While a pre-nuptial agreement will address what happens to property if the parties divorce, it will also talk about division of property when one of them passes away. Most commonly, the parties want to keep the property they brought into the marriage, and to divide the property they bought together.

The agreements can be quite detailed at times, even listing individual items of furniture or jewelry, and this is usually a good thing in terms of estate planning. When there is an agreement between two parties that one will take certain specified items on the death of the other, but will not take certain other specified items, it adds certainty to the division of household items and larger assets as well.

This is not to say that having a pre-nuptial agreement means that you don't need a will. It is not a substitute for a will, though it can be a good supplement to a will.

There are parts of a will that are simply not addressed in a pre-nuptial agreement, such as the appointment of an executor or trusts for minor children. You still need a will even with a pre-nuptial agreement.

These days, pre-nuptial agreements are often used when people enter into second marriages. This is not because they don't trust the new spouse, or that they think the marriage will fail, though in some places there is still some stigma attached to them. The greatest motivator for individuals in second marriages to have pre-nuptial agreements is to ensure that the assets gained during the first marriage end up in the hands of the children of the first marriage.

It is important to understand the parameters of your pre-nuptial agreement. There are certain things it can do for you in terms of estate planning, but it has its limits as well. Make sure you know what all of the clauses mean.

One clause that frequently causes problems in estate matters is the one that says that the spouses each agree not to make a claim against the estate of the other. There is nothing wrong with the clause as far as it goes, but many individuals believe it means more than it actually does. This invariably makes someone think that there is now no way that the spouse can get anything from the estate, but that is not necessarily what it means. It says that the spouse will not *make a claim*; it does not say that the spouse waives any rights that already exist without needing to make a claim.

For example, in Chapter 5 there is a section that discusses the home that a couple lives in and refers to as their matrimonial home. It explains that in some jurisdictions, when one spouse owns the home they share together and that spouse passes away, the surviving spouse automatically has the right to own the property. This is important because the spouse doesn't have to make a claim to get that right. It arises automatically. This means that the statement that the spouse won't make a claim does not interfere with the spouse getting the house.

This can often cause problems for the executor of the estate who has been told by his or her parent that the house is going to the children of the first marriage, but finds that the second spouse actually owns the house now.

In cases where certain rights arise automatically, those rights have to be waived specifically. The standard, boilerplate language of a pre-nuptial agreement does not achieve that. It can certainly be done in a pre-nuptial agreement, but it would have to be specifically addressed.

iii. Moving between provinces

All of the laws, regulations, and forms dealing with wills and estates are made by the legislatures of the provinces and territories. In some cases, they vary quite a bit from one part of the country to another. Because of this, you may wonder whether your documents made in one province or territory are still valid if you move across borders.

As a general rule, a will that is valid in one province or territory will be acceptable in another. The requirements for signing and witnessing are so close – if not identical – that there is rarely an issue with validity arising from the formalities.

Keep in mind, though, that there are differences in law across the provinces that might have an impact on how effective your will is going to be. For example, all provinces have laws that deal with the matrimonial home but they are not the same everywhere. As another example, Henson Trusts are valid everywhere in Canada except for Alberta. Also, in some provinces marriage revokes a will while in others it does not. So while you may take comfort in the fact that moving to a new place may not invalidate your will, it is a very good idea to see a lawyer in your new province or territory to review your will and see if it is still effective in your new jurisdiction.

Enduring Powers of Attorney do not cross provincial or territorial borders very well at all. They have such different forms, signing requirements, and methods of bringing them into effect that they are next to worthless in practical terms once you move to a new province. Be sure to visit a lawyer in your new province or territory to review your Enduring Power of Attorney and health care directive to ensure that you have the appropriate documents in place.

B. Accountant

Though estate planning lawyers know the basics of tax law, they are not experts in taxation the way some accountants are. Clients who want specific or complex tax advice should consult an accountant as well as a lawyer. Not all accountants do the same kind of work, of course, so you will have to find an accountant who is familiar with taxation, preferably as it relates to estates.

i. Business valuation

One of the ways in which accountants are invaluable during estate planning is advising of the value of a privately-owned business. Particularly where a small business is incorporated, it will have its taxes prepared annually by an accountant, who will usually prepare a full set of financial documents each year.

Having your financials prepared by an accountant is not the same thing as having a certified business valuator examine your business. However, most small business owners don't seem to use business valuators unless they are in the process of trying to sell their business. For most purposes, they can gain the information they need about the value of their business from the financial statements prepared by their lawyers.

Knowing the value of your business is essential during estate planning, for several reasons. Shares of a privately-owned business are capital property and therefore subject to capital gains tax. Knowing the value of the shares helps the business owner decide whether he or she should have life insurance to cover the buy-back of the shares left to a beneficiary in the will.

It is also a good idea to know the value of something you are leaving to one person, if you also want to try to leave other beneficiaries gifts of equal value. This is a scenario that faces many business owners who want to leave their business to one of their children. They want to treat all of the children equally, so they need to know the value of the business.

    ii.   **Estate freeze**

Accountants are also involved in estate freezes. An estate freeze is a process whereby ownership of a business is transferred from the current owner to a new owner, who is usually a child of the current owner. The transfer takes place when the current owner gives up his common shares (these are the shares with voting control) and exchanges them for preferred (non-voting) shares. The preferred shares have a fixed value that is agreed upon by the current and new owners and is generally fixed with the help of the accountant.

The new owner then gets the common shares, and by doing so gets the ownership and control of the company. Instead of paying the full cost of buying the company all at once, the new owner agrees to redeem the old owner's preferred shares over time. Each year, the old owner cashes in a few of the preferred shares. This provides the old owner with income, and gives the new owner a break because he or she doesn't have to come up with the full purchase price all at one time.

This transaction is called a "freeze" because it freezes the value of the preferred shares. This is done so that the old owner's capital gains tax liability is fixed, and never increases. If the company continues to prosper and goes up in value, any tax owing on the increase belongs to the new owner.

Example:

A: Before the freeze:
- iii. Jim owns 100% of the common shares of JimCo.
- iv. The company is worth $1,000,000.
- v. Jim wants to sell his company to his daughter, Mary.

B: During the freeze:
- vi.   Jim gives the common shares to Mary.
- vii.   Jim gets new, preferred shares in exchange.
- viii.   The value of the preferred shares is $1,000,000.
- ix.   Jim pays capital gains tax from the day he started the company to the day of the freeze.

C: After the freeze:
- x.   Mary owns the common shares of JimCo. worth $1,000,000.
- xi.   JimCo owes Jim $1,000,000.
- xii.   Each year Jim gives back 1 preferred share and receives a set sum of money. This continues each year until Jim has received $1,000,000 from JimCo.
- xiii.   Any tax arising on the company after the freeze date is paid by Mary.

C. Financial advisor

Your financial advisor or money manager is the person who is most familiar with your assets, your liabilities, and your future plans. Most individuals who are not business owners don't regularly work with accountants other than getting their annual tax return completed, but do work regularly with someone who will help advise them on how to make the most of their current and future assets.

A financial advisor can be very helpful before, during, and after the will-planning process because he or she will help you arrange your finances to avoid excessive taxation, and to take advantage of legal options such as spousal rollovers of capital property. When an individual's personal finances are complicated, sometimes the financial advisor will accompany the individual to the meeting with the lawyer to answer questions about assets. However, your financial advisor should not be preparing your will himself or herself.

i. Recommend your POA use your advisor

An idea that is becoming more popular is to suggest in your Enduring Power of Attorney that the person acting as your attorney continue to use the same financial advisor that you have been using. If you have been working with one advisor for some time and have built a trusting relationship, consider putting a statement in your document that your named attorney continue to work with that person you trust. After all, that advisor knows your goals, your risk tolerance, your income, and your assets. Some people gain peace of mind knowing that their attorney will have someone reliable and trustworthy to turn to for guidance, particularly if the named attorney is one of their children.

CHAPTER 10: PROBATE

Probate is a court process that takes place after a person has passed away, so there may be some dispute about whether a discussion of probate belongs in a book about planning estates before death. The topic of probate is discussed here because many people believe that avoiding probate is a goal they should actively pursue during the planning stage. Thousands of individuals make serious estate-planning mistakes because they are misinformed about probate process, probate costs, and steps to avoiding probate. Those individuals almost never find out about their mistakes, leaving the mess behind for their families to sort out.

In this chapter you will gain a basic understanding of what is involved in applying for probate so that you can judge for yourself whether it is actually important to try to set up your affairs to avoid probate. There is a chart in this chapter that shows the cost of probate in all provinces and territories in Canada. This is important because there is a lot of misinformation out there about the supposedly sky-high cost of probate. As with any decisions, it is better and more effective to have the facts first.

This chapter will also take a look at some of the steps people take in order to avoid probate, and will point out some of the pitfalls of those steps.

A. Facts about probate

Probate is a court process in which an executor named in a will asks the court to declare that the will is valid and that he or she may proceed with the estate as set out in the documents. The executor supports his or her request with a package of documents that include a full inventory of the estate and details about the deceased's family. The court then issues an order which is called a Grant of Probate or Letters Probate.

All provinces and territories in Canada follow this procedure except for Quebec. Their system does not require wills that were prepared by Notaries to be probated.

Once the court has issued the grant of probate, the executor may use the grant to gain access to the deceased's assets and to transfer the deceased's property. Because the grant of probate is an order of the court, everyone who follows it in good faith is indemnified by it. For example, if a land titles registry relied on a valid grant of probate to transfer title of a deceased person's home to a buyer, the land registry cannot be held liable for the transfer if it turns out later that it was not a bona fide buyer.

Not every will needs to be probated. The executor gains his or her authority from the will and may begin work on the estate without getting probate. If the assets are small, the executor may be able to take care of the entire estate without going through probate.

Certain types of assets are always going to require the executor to apply for probate, regardless of their value. One such asset is real estate. The land titles registry wants the indemnity of the court order before changing the title belonging to someone else. If you own a piece of real estate in your own name, no matter how large or small the value, the land titles registry will require a grant of probate before they will allow your executor to change the title.

In other cases, probate is required because of the value of an asset. For example, a large bank account or investment portfolio held with a money manager will require probate in order for an executor to cash it in. This is because the bank or money manager wants the indemnity provided by the court order. If a bank releases an account worth $50,000 to a person who claims to be an executor but who is not, the bank is liable to the estate for that $50,000. If, however, the bank has relied on the proof offered by a grant of probate that the executor is who he or she says she is, the bank would not be liable for paying out the account.

The higher the value of an asset, the more likely it is that the executor is going to have to obtain probate in order to cash or collect the asset. When the only asset in an estate is a small account with a few thousand dollars, the bank may agree to release the account without the executor going through probate, but this is not going to happen with a large account.

Sometimes an executor needs to apply for probate of a will for reasons that have nothing to do with the type or value of assets. In such cases, it is usually because there is some question about the will that the executor wants the court to look at and clarify. For example, the will might not be dated, or there could be words that could be read two ways. When the executor needs interpretation or clarification of a will, sometimes it can be done at the same time as the probate application to save time and money. Executors can't simply decide what an executor "really meant" if the will is not clear. Only a judge can do that.

An executor might also file for probate if there is someone in the estate who has the right to bring a claim and the executor wants to bring an end to the claim period. For example, a spouse of the deceased has a certain amount of time (usually six months) from the date of the probate to bring a claim for a greater share of the estate. If the executor does not apply for probate then the claim period never starts running, and therefore it never ends. That means that the executor could not distribute the estate. Therefore the executor would probably choose to obtain probate for procedural purposes.

When all of the documents are filed at the court, a request for probate usually takes about three or four weeks to be processed by the courts. At times there are backlogs but normally there is not a long wait for the order.

Summary:
Whether a particular will requires probate is based on:
- The type of asset in the estate;
- The value of assets in the estate;
- How assets are held (e.g. jointly, solely);
- Requirements of local registries;
- Requirements of banks and investment companies;
- Disputes among beneficiaries;
- Questions about the validity of the will.

B. The cost of probate

Whenever an executor files a request for probate, he or she must pay a fee to the court. The fee varies widely across the country but are generally related to the value of the estate that is being probated. There is no GST or HST added to the fee. If an executor has access to the deceased's bank accounts before he or she applies for probate, the fee may legitimately be paid from the deceased's funds as it is an expense of the estate. In reality, some executors cannot gain access to the accounts prior to obtaining probate and end up paying the court fee themselves. If this happens, they may reimburse themselves as soon as estate funds become available.

Table 6: *Cost of probate across Canada*

Province or territory	Cost of Letters Probate
Alberta	$35 for an estate of $10,000 or less
	$135 for an estate over $10,000 up to $25,000
	$275 for an estate over $25,000 up to $125,000
	$400 for an estate over $125,000 up to $250,000
	$525 for an estate over $250,000

British Columbia	No fee if the estate is less than $25,000

For the portion of the gross value over $25,000 up to $50,000, fee is 0.6%

For the portion of the gross value over $50,000, the fee is 1.4% |
| Manitoba | $70 up to the first $10,000

For any portion over $10,000, fee is 0.7% |
| New Brunswick | $25 for estate of $5,000 or less

$50 for estates over $5,000 up to $10,000

$75 for estates over $10,000 up to $15,000

$100 for estates over $15,000 up to $20,000

For estates over $20,000, the fee is 0.5% |
| Newfoundland & Labrador | $60 for the first $1,000

For portion of the estate over $1,000, the fee is 0.6% |

Northwest Territories	$25 for estates of $10,000 or less

$100 for over $10,000 up to $25,000

$200 for over $25,000 up to $125,000

$300 for over $125,000 up to $250,000

$400 for over $250,000 |
| Nova Scotia | $83.10 for estates with a value of $10,000 or less

$208.95 for over $10,000 up to $25,000

$347.70 for over $25,000 up to $50,000

$973.45 for over $50,000 up to $100,000

Where an estate is more than $100,000, the fee is $973.45 for the first $100,000 and then 1.645% on the rest |

Nunavut	$25 for estate with net value of $10,000 or under

$100 for more than $10,000 and up to $25,000

$200 for more than $25,000 and up to $125,000

$300 for more than $125,000 and up to $250,000

$400 for more than $250,000 |
| Ontario | No fee if the estate is less than $1,000

0.5% on the first $50,000

1.5% on the amount over $50,000 |
| Prince Edward Island | $50 if the estate is $10,000 or less

$100 for over $10,000 up to $25,000
$200 for over $25,000 up to $50,000

$400 for over $50,000 up to $100,000

If the estate is more than $100,000, the fee is $400 for first $100,000, then 0.4% on |

	the rest.
Quebec	$105 for a natural person

$118 for a legal person

Note that in Quebec, these are court filing fees for verification of wills. There are no probate fees. |
| Saskatchewan | For all estates, the fee is 0.7% |
| Yukon | $140 for an estate with a value of $25,000 or more.

Estates below $25,000 may or may not be charged a fee. |

C. Avoiding probate

There are probably more mistakes made by well-meaning individuals who are trying to avoid probate than there are as a result of any other goal. Unfortunately, people hear stories or read articles and only know a small bit of the story. They hear bits and pieces in which complex and tangled situations are boiled down into a few nuggets of information. Rarely are they advised of the pitfalls of probate avoidance techniques, and even if they are advised, they may not realize how those pitfalls pertain to them.

If you have been advised to try to avoid probate, or you have read articles or blog posts about it, do not take that at face value. Look into it further and make sure you know all the facts before you go ahead.

First of all, evaluate the source of your information. If you have simply heard of probate avoidance from friends, family, or co-workers, remember that they are not lawyers. Don't take legal advice from friends, bankers, real estate agents, or anyone else who is not a lawyer. When reading articles online, find out whether the information is actually intended for your geographic region, whether it's up to date, and whether the person writing the information actually has the qualifications to give the advice you're reading. Protect yourself and your family by backing up anything you've heard or read by asking a qualified lawyer.

D. Why avoid probate?

Assuming you are interested in learning more about avoiding probate, your first question should be "why?" Why do you want to avoid having your will go through probate? How would avoiding probate help you or your family? Would it save money? Would it make things easier? Don't simply assume that it would do either of these things, even if you know of cases where it did save money or did smooth the way. Your family and your situation are not the same as anyone else's, so make sure you know how avoiding probate would be of use to you.

Many people assume that setting up their financial and legal affairs to avoid probate will save their estate money. However, this may be completely untrue if you live in a province in which the probate fees are low. Check the previous sections of this chapter to see how much probate fees will be in your province or territory. Then, balance those fees against the cost of changing titles now, and against the potential cost of legal fees should there be a problem with your estate. Perhaps your plan isn't as cost-effective as you thought.

Many, many families find out too late that the steps they took to save money actually ended up costing them more because their arrangements created confusion that needed to be cleared up by the courts.

Earlier in this book, we talked about setting some estate planning goals. Perhaps you believe that avoiding probate should be among your goals, and perhaps you're right. However, do not pursue the avoidance of probate to the exclusion of your other goals or to the point that avoiding probate creates new problems and costs. Avoiding probate should be secondary to goals such as protecting children and ensuring that your spouse is provided for.

Keep in mind that regardless of the steps you take now to avoid probate, you cannot guarantee that your will is not going to need to be probated. There are variables that you cannot control in advance. For example, you cannot control the policies about probate requirements set up by banks.

E. Weighing the risks against the benefits

By far the most common advice given to people who want to avoid probate is to place some or all of their assets into joint names with their children. At this point in time, the idea of placing assets in joint names is so widespread across Canada that it is simply being talked about in back yards and over coffee, rather than in lawyers' offices.

Unfortunately, adding your children to your assets is not an effective way to avoid probate, as is discussed in some detail in previous chapters of this book. In addition to the simple fact that the strategy simply does not work, there are enormous risks and downsides to arranging your assets this way.

When a parent adds a child's name to a property owned by the parent, he or she is handing over ownership of the property immediately. While parents usually think that they are handing over *future* ownership –upon the death of the parents - the fact is that joint ownership means the child owns the property now just as much as the parent does. To many parents, the concept of adding a child to the title means that nothing happens immediately but upon their death, things change. They are completely wrong. Things change immediately. Adding the child as an owner means that the child can prevent the parent from selling or mortgaging the property. It also means that if the child should get divorced, the parent's home could well be lost in the child's matrimonial property division. Most parents can't afford that.

In any situation in which the child might be sued, such as a car accident or a business failure, the parent's home is on the line. Each time an additional child's name is added, the parent's risk is multiplied. Parents think of the procedure as simply "adding a name" but it is really handing over ownership and control of a major asset to someone else. Most people take it much too lightly, given the legal issues and the value of the asset.

In addition to the risk of losing the parent's home, adding a child may also create a tax liability that did not exist before. For example, let's say that Fred is widowed and owns his house. It's worth $300,000 now, but he bought it years ago for $60,000. Fred has two kids, Sarah and Emily, each of whom is grown up and living with their own families in their own homes.

Fred's home is his principal residence, so if he were to pass away while his home is in his own name only, there would be no capital gains tax on the sale.

However, Fred reads an article that talks about adding his children to the title of his home, and adds Sarah and Emily's names to his house. Now, only Fred's share of the house – one third – is going to be tax free on sale. The portions of the house that belong to the children are taxable.

Here's the difference:

In Fred's name only:

$300,000	value of house on sale
$ -60,000	adjusted cost base of house
$240,000	capital gain
$-240,000	principal residence exemption
$ 0	tax on the sale

In the name of Fred, Sarah, and Emily:

$300,000	value of house on sale
$ -60,000	adjusted cost base of house
$240,000	capital gain

$-80,000   principal residence exemption (Fred's 1/3 of
             the house)
$160,000   tax on the sale

Fred has created a new tax liability for his estate of $160,000 by adding his children's name to the house. This means his children will inherit that much less. In an attempt to avoid the cost of probate, Fred has created a bill much larger than anything he would have been charged for probate. For comparison purposes, let's look at what probate fees would be on a house worth $300,000:

Province or territory	Cost of Letters Probate for an estate of $300,000
Alberta	$525
British Columbia	$3,650
Manitoba	$2,100
New Brunswick	$1,500
Newfoundland & Labrador	$1,859.64
Northwest Territories	$400
Nova Scotia	$4,263.45
Nunavut	$400
Ontario	$4,000
Prince Edward Island	$1,200
Quebec	$105
Saskatchewan	$2,100
Yukon	$140

As you can clearly see, there is no jurisdiction in Canada that has a probate fee even close to the tax liability that Fred has created by adding his children's names to his home. His estate is going to be reduced by a significant amount for no good reason. Anyone who is considering adding their children's names to their home to avoid probate fees is encouraged to crunch the actual numbers this way to get the facts and see what the real outcome would be for them.

F. Survivorship presumptions

In several places in this book, we have talked about a beneficiary surviving the person who made the will. That may make it sound as if it is always easy to tell who died first and to whom an inheritance should flow. However, in real life there may be a question about that, such as when two people, say a married couple, are in an accident together and there is no way to tell who died first.

The question becomes important in the context of wills because a husband and wife often make wills that leave everything they own to each other. This leaves the family in a quandary as to who actually is supposed to inherit from whom.

The law has an answer to the question, of course. Traditionally, the law has said that when there is a question about who died first in a common accident, the younger of the two is deemed to have survived. The estate of the older half of the married couple would all go to the younger of the two, and then would be distributed according to the younger person's will, or in the absence of a will, according to the local law of intestacy.

This might not be a problem if the deceased couple had children and they had mirror wills in which both of them left everything to each other. But in the case where there are no children, the operation of law means that the entire estate is going to go to the parents, siblings, or other relatives of the younger person.

For example, let's say Jared and Rebecca are married and have no children. They are involved in a car crash while on vacation together, and by the time paramedics arrive, both have passed away so that it's not possible to know who died first. Because Rebecca was younger, the law presumes that she survived Jared. She doesn't have a will, so the law follows the provincial law of intestacy. Her parents are not alive, so the entire estate is divided between her siblings. This is upsetting to Jared's parents since they were the ones who gave the couple $40,000 for a down payment on their home.

As with many areas of estate law, recent updates are beginning to change the old ways of doing things. The newer way of thinking is that in a case like Rebecca and Jared, the estate would be split equally between their two families. However, changes to the law come slowly and this is not yet the law everywhere.

The table below shows how the various provinces and territories deal with the question of who survived whom in a common accident. When talking about who survived whom, the law is called a "survivorship presumption". This means that in the absence of evidence, the law will presume that things happened a certain way. Because it is a presumption and not a fact, evidence can be brought (if there is any) to overcome the presumption.

Table 7: *Survivorship presumptions in all provinces and territories in Canada*

Province or territory	Survivorship presumption when a married couple dies in a common accident
Alberta	Each of them will be presumed to have died before the other, unless the Will states a contrary intention. Each person's estate will pass to his or her alternate beneficiaries. Any property held by the deceased individuals as joint tenants will be deemed to be held as tenants in common, so a one-half interest will pass to each person's estate.
British Columbia	Each of them will be presumed to have died before the other, unless the Will states a contrary intention. Each person's estate will pass to his or her alternate beneficiaries. Any property held by the deceased individuals as joint tenants will be deemed to be held as tenants in common, so a one-half interest will pass to each person's estate.

Manitoba	Each of them will be presumed to have died before the other, unless the Will states a contrary intention. Each person's estate will pass to his or her alternate beneficiaries. Any property held by the deceased individuals as joint tenants will be deemed to be held as tenants in common, so a one-half interest will pass to each person's estate.
New Brunswick	Each of them will be presumed to have died before the other, unless the Will states a contrary intention. Each person's estate will pass to his or her alternate beneficiaries. Any property held by the deceased individuals as joint tenants will be deemed to be held as tenants in common, so a one-half interest will pass to each person's estate.
Newfoundland & Labrador	The younger person is deemed to have survived the older person. All goes to the estate of the younger person.
Northwest Territories	The younger person is deemed to have survived the older person. All goes to the estate of the younger person.

Nova Scotia	The younger person is deemed to have survived the older person. All goes to the estate of the younger person.
Nunavut	The younger person is deemed to have survived the older person. All goes to the estate of the younger person.
Ontario	Each of them will be presumed to have died before the other, unless the Will states a contrary intention. Each person's estate will pass to his or her alternate beneficiaries. Any property held by the deceased individuals as joint tenants will be deemed to be held as tenants in common, so a one-half interest will pass to each person's estate.
Prince Edward Island	The younger person is deemed to have survived the older person. All goes to the estate of the younger person.
Quebec	They will be deemed to have died at the same time. Each person's estate will pass to his or her alternate beneficiaries.

Saskatchewan	Each of them will be presumed to have died before the other, unless the Will states a contrary intention. If they die within 5 days of each other, they are considered to have died at the same time.
Yukon	Each of them will be presumed to have died before the other, unless the Will states a contrary intention. Each person's estate will pass to his or her alternate beneficiaries. Any property held by the deceased individuals as joint tenants will be deemed to be held as tenants in common, so a one-half interest will pass to each person's estate.

CONCLUSION

After looking through this book, you should feel much more prepared to go ahead with your estate planning than you did before. No doubt you will refer back to this book many times as you learn of new ideas and gain new information. If you already have estate planning and capacity documents in place, you can use this book to review them to get an idea of whether they need to be brought up to date.

This is meant to be a practical guide, so we always appreciate feedback. If you have comments about this book, suggestions for topics for inclusion in future editions, or questions about anything you've read in this book, please feel free to email the author at lynne@butlerwillsandestates.com. We will always do our best to respond to emails quickly.

If you wish to look further into any topic you've seen in this book, a good starting place is the author's blog at www.estatelawcanada.blogspot.ca.

Lynne Butler is a practicing lawyer and welcomes new clients who are looking for services relating to wills, estates, probate, powers of attorney, or mediation of estate disputes. Her office can be reached at 709-221-5511. Services and prices are listed on her webpage at www.butlerwillsandestates.com.

ESTATE PLANNING WORKSHEET

This worksheet is a place for you to gather your information and your thoughts. It is not a will, but it's a good starting point if you are thinking of having a will and/or incapacity documents made.

Not all questions will apply to you. Fill in those that do, and make a few notes about questions you want to ask. If you plan to see a lawyer, it's a good idea to fill out the Worksheet by hand, and take it to your meeting.

Information about you:

Your full name:
_____

Any aliases or previous names:
_____

Address:
_____

Phone:
_____

Email:
_____

Date of birth:
_____

Place of birth:
_____

Citizenship:
_____

Social insurance number:
_____

Place of employment:
_____

Information about your family:

Your spouse's name:
_____

Are you legally married or common law?
_____

When did you marry or move in together?
_____

Spouse's date of birth:
_____

Were you previously married or in a common law relationship? If so, former spouse's name:
_____

Date the previous relationship ended:
_____

Record the following information about each of your children:
Name _____
Date of birth _____
Marital status _____
Whether they have children _____

Name _____
Date of birth _____
Marital status _____
Whether they have children _____

Name _____
Date of birth _____
Marital status _____
Whether they have children _____

Name _____
Date of birth _____
Marital status _____
Whether they have children _____

Which, if any, of your children are adopted, step-children, or from a previous relationship?
_____

Are any of the children disabled mentally or physically?
_____

What is the nature or cause of the disability?
_____

Are you currently paying spousal support to anyone?
_____

Are you currently paying child support to anyone?
_____

Information about your finances – real estate:

Your home:
Address:
_____

How is the title held (i.e. by one person only, jointly, tenants in common)?
_____

Is there an amount outstanding on the mortgage?
_____

Net value of the property:
_____

Cabin or cottage:
Address:
_____

How is the title held?
_____

Is there an amount outstanding on the mortgage?
_____

When did you buy or build it?
_____

Were improvements made, and if so, what did they cost?
_____

Net value of the property:
_____

Rental properties that you own:
Address #1:
_____

How is the title held?
_____

Is there a mortgage?
_____

When did you buy it?
_____

Net value of the property:
_____

Address #2:
_____

How is the title held?
_____

Is there a mortgage?
_____

When did you buy it?
_____

Net value of the property:
_____

Financial Information – other assets

Bank accounts
Do you have a bank account that is only in your name?
_____

Do you have a bank account jointly with your spouse?
_____

Do you have a bank account jointly with anyone else? If so, why?
_____

Which bank do you use?
_____

Non-registered Investments:
Do you have non-registered investments only in your name?
_____

Do you have non-registered investments jointly with your spouse?
_____

Do you have non-registered investments held jointly with anyone else?
_____

RRSP
At which bank is your RRSP held?
_____

Who is named as the beneficiary of your RRSP?
_____

Does your spouse have an RRSP? At which bank?

_____

Who is the beneficiary of your spouse's RRSP?

_____

RRIF
At which bank is your RRIF held?

_____

Amount in the RRIF:

_____

Who is named as the beneficiary of your RRIF?

_____

Does your spouse have a RRIF? At which bank?

_____

Amount in your spouse's RRIF:

_____

Who is the beneficiary of your spouse's RRIF?

_____

Pension:
Are you eligible for federal government pension benefits (OAP, CPP)?

_____

Are you eligible for a pension from your employer or former employer, or any other private source?

_____
_____
_____

Are you eligible for a pension from another country?
_____

Who is the beneficiary of your pension?
_____

Life insurance:
For each life insurance policy owned by you or your spouse, fill in the following information:

Insurance company:
_____

Face value of policy
_____

Beneficiary of policy
_____

Insurance company:
_____

Face value of policy
_____

Beneficiary of policy
_____

Does anyone owe you money? If so, explain:
_____
_____
_____
_____
_____

Business assets:
Do you own a business or part of a business?
_____

What is the name of the business?
_____

Is it incorporated?
_____

What percentage of the business do you own?
_____

Who else owns a share of the business?
_____
_____
_____

What is the value of your share of the business?
_____

When did you acquire your shares?
_____

Is there a signed Shareholders' Agreement in place?
_____

Other assets (e.g. vehicles, boats, collections, artwork):

Please list other assets and their value:
_____
_____
_____
_____

***Beneficiaries*:**

If your spouse outlives you, do you want him/her to receive your whole estate?
_____

If not, what arrangement do you suggest?
_____
_____
_____
_____
_____

Do you wish to leave specific personal items to certain people?
_____
_____
_____
_____
_____

Do you intend to leave a Memorandum of Personal Effects?
_____

Do you want all of your children to inherit equally from you?
_____

If not, what arrangement do you suggest?
_____
_____
_____
_____
_____

Why do you want your children to receive different amounts?

_____
_____
_____
_____

At what age (or ages) should your children receive their inheritance?

_____
_____
_____

Should your children's guardians have access to funds held in trust for your children before the children come of age (for example, for medical care or education expenses, or simply for regular living expenses)?

_____
_____
_____
_____

If one of your children predeceased you, what should happen to their share of your estate?

_____
_____
_____
_____

Have you made loans to any of your children?

_____
_____
_____

Have you helped any of your children financially?

_____
_____
_____

Do you want those loans or advances taken into account or forgiven?
_____
_____

Do you currently have any joint accounts or joint property with your children? If yes, which assets?
_____
_____
_____

Why were their names added to your account or property?
_____
_____
_____
_____

Do you want the child who is the joint owner of your assets to keep those assets for him/herself, or to divide them among all of your children?
_____
_____

Personal Representatives:

Who would you appoint as executor?
_____

Who would you appoint as alternate executor, in case your first choice isn't able or willing to do it?
_____

How much should your executor be paid?
_____

Who would you appoint as guardian for any of your children who are minors when you pass away?
_____

Who would you appoint as alternate guardian?
_____

Power of Attorney:

Who would you appoint under your Power of Attorney to make financial decisions for you if can no longer do that for yourself?
_____

Who would you appoint as alternate?
_____

Who should have the legal authority to spring your POA into effect?
_____

Special instructions:
_____
_____
_____
_____
_____
_____

Advance Health Care Directive:

Who would you appoint as your agent under an Advance Health Care Directive to make personal and medical decisions for you if you can no longer do that for yourself?
_____

Who would you appoint as alternate?
_____

What are your wishes regarding being kept alive artificially?
_____
_____
_____

Are you willing to allow your organs or tissue to be used for transplant to help someone else?
_____

Special instructions regarding health or personal care:
_____
_____
_____
_____
_____

Questions or topics to discuss with your lawyer:
_____
_____
_____
_____
_____

More books by Lynne Butler

To purchase these titles, go to
www.newfoundlandlawbooks.com

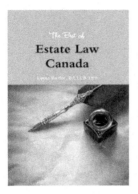

The Best of Estate Law Canada

Lynne's blog has been read by more than 4 million people so far. This books sorts the 80 most-read posts from her blog into topics, updates them, and adds commentary, so that you can have the most essential information all in one handy place!

The Beneficiary's Answer Book

This book answers 175 of the questions asked most often by beneficiaries. It covers topics such as probate, tax, power of executors, time line for estates, beneficiaries' rights, and much more.

Cinderella's Trust Fund

Serious legal information can be fun to read, as you'll see in this book that uses fairy tales and nursery rhymes as jumping off points for estate planning topics.

Sound Mind and Memory: 19th Century Newfoundland Wills

This book looks at what we can learn about 19th century Newfoundland through the wills left behind by her people. It's a balance of history, law, culture, and entertaining anecdotes.

For My Family, With Love

A comprehensive workbook to hold info about assets, contacts, passwords, personal messages and more to help your family after you've passed away. Also an essential tool for anyone acting under a Power of Attorney.

How Executors Avoid Personal Liability

A detailed guidebook to executor's duties, with info about avoiding common mistakes and realistic tips for getting the job done right.

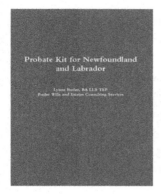

Probate Kit for Newfoundland and Labrador

This kit contains all of the forms needed to apply for probate in NL, with detailed instructions for completion and filing at the court. Includes a comprehensive printed guide and forms on flash drive.

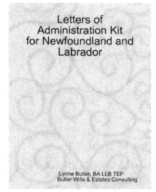

Letters of Administration Kit for Newfoundland and Labrador

Everything you need to apply to become the administrator of an estate in NL is in this kit. This is suitable when the deceased left no will, or when there is a will with no executor, or when you need to take over from an executor who didn't finish the job. Contains a comprehensive printed guide, and a USB drive with all necessary forms.

Note: The two kits shown on this page are only available at www.butlerwillsandestates.com or by calling 709-221-5511.